Project Research in Information Systems

Project Research in Information Systems

A Student's Guide

Second Edition

Tony Cornford
Steve Smithson
Department of Information Systems
London School of Economics and Political Science

First edition 1996
Reprinted twelve times
Second edition 2006

Published by
PALGRAVE MACMILLAN
Houndmills, Basingstoke, Hampshire RG21 6XS and
175 Fifth Avenue, New York, N.Y. 10010
Companies and representatives throughout the world.

PALGRAVE MACMILLAN is the global academic imprint of the Palgrave Macmillan division of St. Martin's Press, LLC and of Palgrave Macmillan Ltd. Macmillan® is a registered trademark in the United States, United Kingdom and other countries. Palgrave is a registered trademark in the European Union and other countries.

ISBN-13: 978–1–4039–3471–0
ISBN-10: 1–4039–3471–1

This book is printed on paper suitable for recycling and made from fully managed and sustained forest sources.

A catalogue record for this book is available from the British Library.

A catalog record for this book is available from the Library of Congress.

10 9 8 7 6 5 4 3 2 1
15 14 13 12 11 10 09 08 07 06

Printed and bound in China

It is beyond the power of the human intellect to encompass all the causes of any phenomenon. But the impulse to search into causes is inherent in man's very nature. And so the human intellect, without investigating the multiplicity and complexity of circumstances conditioning any event, any one of which taken separately may seem to be the reason for it, snatches at the most comprehensible approximation to a cause and says: 'There is the cause!'

War and Peace, Leo Tolstoy

Contents

Preface

This book has been written to help students undertaking research projects within taught information systems courses, and the main intended audience are final-year undergraduates and students taking taught masters degrees. For these students the book offers a clear and comprehensive account of how to successfully undertake project work. The book can also provide a useful starting point for people commencing on more substantial research activity, for example, PhD or MPhil studies. At this level most institutions will provide some formal teaching in research methodology, and while this book is not meant as a textbook for such courses, it does provide a readable introduction to many of the substantive issues.

When considering project work the level of study is perhaps not so critical; while expectations and assessment criteria may vary, and would in general be higher for postgraduate work, all students undertaking their own research projects at whatever stage in their education share the same core concerns; they must choose and refine a topic, plan and organize their research, carry it out using appropriate techniques, and write it up in a coherent and well structured report. These are the concerns of this book, addressed in a concise, thoughtful and pragmatic fashion.

The case for projects

The widespread use of computer-based information systems throughout industry, government and society, and the resulting changes in the demand for relevant skills and expertise have resulted in a significant increase in the number of information systems, computing and related courses that are offered in higher education. These courses are offered in a number of different forms and styles, ranging from those drawing principally on management themes, such as undergraduate degrees in business administration and MBAs, to courses reflecting a more technical perspective, for example, in applied software engineering. There are also increasing numbers of more focused courses, such as undergraduate degrees in e-commerce or Masters degrees in web engineering, as well as programmes within the social sciences, such as media studies, that directly address information systems concerns.

This book is intended as a useful resource for all such students and its fundamental message about the information systems field, the research focus it develops and the practical guidance it offers can easily be translated across these disciplinary boundaries. A *common* interest in information and communication technology, as it is developed and shaped, applied and used, and the consequences that follow, provides the strong unifying focus. Furthermore, the deep-seated economic and social changes brought about in our world by the adoption of information and communication technology makes carrying out student research projects a particularly appropriate and effective way to learn. Projects thus offer the opportunity to become directly engaged with these changes going on in the world, and to start to appreciate them at first hand. If we understand information systems as typically involving the interaction of people (managers, employees, consumers, patients etc.) and information and communication technologies within a particular context (a business organization, government department, hospital etc.), and in support of some particular task or activity, then it should be clear that it is often appropriate to study such situations at first hand and through direct observation and by interaction with the people involved. In this way the ideas and models found in textbooks and taught in formal courses, can be tested against what actually happens in the 'real' world, and students can develop a far more grounded understanding of their field.

Problems with projects

We have made the strong pedagogical case for project work as a way to deepen learning, but our experience suggests that many students find it difficult to undertake, and do not always produce work that reflects their true ability or develops their understanding to the extent possible. They may not even enjoy working on projects. The reasons are various, but here we suggest four main causes:

Scale: The first problem is the perceived scale of the task. Most students have no experience of independently planning, designing and carrying out a large project within a strict deadline. Parts of this text are therefore devoted to providing guidelines for the organization and management of projects.

Skills: A second, closely related, problem is that project work demands the employment of certain research skills in a 'real' and often open-ended situation. These skills include defining an appropriate topic to study, searching the relevant literature, organizing and carrying out particular methods of data collection (interviews, surveys, observation, etc.), analysing the collected data, and writing it up in a well structured report. Students may in theory have learned about some of these skills in their prior studies, but this is probably their first venture into 'the field'. In this book, we provide support for developing these relevant skills, keeping an appropriate balance between theoretical and pragmatic aspects.

Matching expectations: The third problem students face is to understand and respond to the expectations of their particular course, their institution and their teachers. Naturally, the requirements of different institutions vary considerably; for example, between practice-based and theory-based research projects, in terms of length of report, format of presentation and the type of topics for study that are encouraged or discouraged. Students also have to start to understand the biases that any institution will have, towards some ways of doing research, and against others. This book can help here too, providing a student with a map of the territory which helps when working out what type of project will work and will be appreciated within their own institutional setting.

Negotiating disciplinary boundaries: Finally, in writing this book we recognize another difficulty that students face: the inherently multi-disciplinary nature of information systems as a field of study. Students typically start project work on the basis of a quite narrow, specialized, background, be it in management, computer science or sociology. And yet, most project situations develop so as to require a mix of approaches, for example, some technical know-how, but also some organizational understanding. It is thus the case that many students, when engaging in their project work, will need to reach out to other areas of knowledge, search out and read new types of material, and balance a number of not always easily compatible approaches and assumptions. Overall, and as will become apparent in the following chapters, our orientation is towards theory-based work, a position which matches the increased emphasis throughout universities on questions of research methodology, research training and the development of academic and analytical skills. This may not, at first sight, directly help those students working at the practical end of the spectrum, but we would argue that clear research questions, an understanding of the current state of knowledge in an area, thoughtful design of the project work and the ability to justify the approaches used, apply just as much to the more practical type of project.

The prime motivation for writing this book has been our experience in setting-up, supervising and marking student projects. Between us, we have also done our own share of projects as undergraduates, postgraduates and doctoral students, and we continue our careers as active researchers. In addition, we have been external examiners for other universities at all levels from undergraduate to PhD, and have viewed the projects of hundreds of students on courses in information systems, business studies and computing. But perhaps the most influential experience for both of us has been our many years spent advising countless Masters students at the London School of Economics.

From this we have learned some of the essence of what it takes to produce a good project in information systems and this is what we try to present in this book. However, the book can neither set down the requirements of any particular institution or course, nor substitute for the involvement of an experienced and knowledgeable adviser. If we have done our job well, however, the book can provide students with advice and information to help to make their own projects an academic success. Equally importantly, we hope, it can help to make the experience of undertaking a research project personally satisfying.

We also would like to think that the book can serve to encourage teachers and lecturers to adopt a more constructive approach to supervising student projects. With the increased work pressures in higher education there is a danger that student projects may be neglected or downgraded. Yet, it is our experience that a positive approach to projects, particularly in the young discipline of information systems, can be an intellectually and academically satisfying part of a teacher's work.

The pleasure that we have received in working with students, and the education that they have provided us through their project work, leads us to dedicate this book to all our students in the Department of Information Systems at LSE, past, present and future.

Tony Cornford and Steve Smithson

Acknowledgements

The initial inspiration for this book was a Subject Guide for the Information Systems Project course of the University of London External Programme degree in Information Systems and Management. We are very grateful to the External Programme of the University of London for permission to use some material from that publication in this book.

We would also like to thank Godfrey Womudhu-Kyama and Laurence Habib for their help in preparing the manuscript for the first edition of this book.

Introduction

■ **The purpose and value of projects**
■ **Thinking about information systems projects**
■ **Taking a research approach**

The origins or particular focus of degree courses in information systems may vary, but they almost all have one common characteristic: a requirement that students undertake at least one substantial individual project or item of course work. The typical requirement for an undergraduate degree is that one quarter or one fifth of the final year is devoted to such a project. This is usually in addition to other project work that forms a part of taught courses. For taught Masters students, requirements vary considerably, but a project or dissertation that is equal to at least one quarter of the total period of study and marks awarded is normal in the United Kingdom.

Project work then represents a significant component of such courses and provides a vital opportunity for students to display their understanding, energy and creativity, free from the straitjacket of unseen written examinations. Project work also provides an opportunity to break out of the academic environment, and to practise skills and refine understanding in relationship with the wider world. Indeed, project work provides an important opportunity for students to measure the relevance and acuity of what they have been taught against the expectations, constraints and concerns of the 'real' world.

For students undertaking a research degree, the 'project' and its final deliverable in the form of a thesis, becomes almost everything. Two, three or even more years are devoted to its completion, and success is very largely defined in terms of delivering an adequate result in the time available. For these students, perhaps more than for undergraduates or Masters students, success is achieved as much by careful attention to process – what to do and how to do it – as it is by pure intellectual activity or distinctive inspiration and insight.

1

The purpose and value of projects

Whatever course a student is following, and at whatever level, project work should be seen as representing the summit of achievement. It is an opportunity to develop a substantial piece of work, to conduct some original research, and in doing this to integrate and draw on various subjects that have been previously studied as well as on personal experience.

The syllabus for most information systems projects is very simple and open-ended, one might almost say vague. The student is asked to choose an issue, problem or case study from the domain of information systems, to study it, and to write an account of what they discover. There is typically an expectation within taught undergraduate courses that projects will be between 6500 and 8000 words long, with perhaps an upper limit of 12,000 words. For Masters degrees such limits may be rather higher, perhaps even extending to 20,000 words. Some courses may impose a bit more structure on the process, perhaps requiring a phased delivery of work with, for example, a detailed project plan and accompanying literature survey as the first submission, and a subsequent submission of a project report detailing empirical work.

For research degrees the size or scope of a project will naturally be larger, as is the expected deliverable. For the University of London, a PhD thesis in the Faculty of Economics, which covers most of information systems, is expected to be no greater than 100,000 words, and should pass a test that is stated in these terms:

> The thesis must form a distinct contribution to the knowledge of the subject and afford evidence of originality, shown either by the discovery of new facts and/or by the exercise of independent critical power. A full bibliography and references will be required.

Whether we are considering a final year undergraduate project with more modest expectations, or a PhD thesis, such work tends to start with a fairly open-ended statement of what is required. This poses a problem and requires that both the choice of topic and of approach be made with care. Indeed, choosing the right topic and the right approach is perhaps the most significant determinant of success, certainly a poor initial choice can doom a project. A well-chosen topic will allow a student to demonstrate his or her particular skills and insights, and help him or her to stay focused on the task of delving deeper in something specific, rather than skidding across the surface of multiple topics, but more importantly, it will capture the interest of the student, and thereby provide strong personal motivation to do good work.

Students who thereafter work carefully and consistently on their project, whatever its size, should not only be able to achieve good grades at the end, but should also feel that they enjoyed the academic experience and that they have produced a polished product of which they can be proud. Indeed, students studying for taught qualifications in information systems often find their projects particularly useful as an opportunity to test their theoretical understanding against the concerns of the wider community, as well as an opportunity to provide a concrete demonstration of their abilities. It is very satisfying and appropriate that students should leave higher education with more to show than just a degree certificate. Potential employers are often interested in seeing a student's project work, or hearing about it, as solid evidence of intellectual abilities and relevant skills that have been mastered.

Thinking about information systems projects

One of the aims of this book is to help students develop their overall perspective on the discipline of information systems. Developing such a perspective is of critical importance, for without it the subject will always be in danger of fragmenting into isolated islands of partial insight or empty technique. We have to recognize that the phrase 'information systems' is often used in a loose and woolly manner, and that there is still much debate and discussion over what exactly the field encompasses and what its theoretical foundations are (see the Chapter 2). Thus anybody who enters into this field needs to work at achieving a personal understanding of the field, and to locate his or her own position within it. Such a strong personal orientation within the field is of great value in providing the foundation for project work and in enabling student researchers to relate their particular work to the wider intellectual debates that characterize this field.

In this young and fast moving field it is very important that students should develop their own understanding of what it means to take an information systems approach to their work and not, for example, one based largely or solely on concerns or models drawn from either business management or computer science. Put another way, student researchers must keep consciously asking themselves the fundamental question: 'How does my work contribute to the broader understanding of the phenomena of information systems?'

In contrast to such important conceptual concerns, the second aim of the book is to give some good 'advice' to students starting out on project work. As you might expect, this is presented in a more programmatic and sequential manner. The book thus offers suggestions about the kinds of thinking that are needed, and the main steps and activities one needs to go through, in order to select a suitable research project and then to bring it to a successful conclusion. We identify this as advice rather than prescription because there can be no simple and universal answers applicable in every case. Each student has to address his or her own project in the specific context of his or her own abilities, the area of study chosen, resources that are available, the research approach to be taken and the requirements of their particular course.

For this reason, in writing this book, we have tried to explain our recommendations and to justify our suggestions, but circumstances will dictate that at times the advice offered will not be compatible with your own situation and will need to be modified or even rejected. Certainly, in every case, the advice given will need to be tailored to a particular situation. We offer it then in the spirit of Checkland's definition of a methodology: 'A set of principles of method which in any particular situation has to be reduced to a method uniquely suited to that particular situation' (Checkland, 1981).

The book also contains a third category of what we term 'useful information', mostly of a practical nature. Thus, some sections give very concrete suggestions as to how to go about specific tasks; for example, how to search a library catalogue, design a questionnaire or collect and cite references. While these aspects of the book may seem to some readers obvious, mundane, pedantic or over specific, it is a happy (and rare) student who has all the answers to all these detailed points. It is also a very rare project that is beyond criticism in such matters, and the overall effect of well-conceived work can all too easily be spoiled by poor and idiosyncratic execution or presentation.

This book then contains a mixture of useful information, advice on process and theoretical perspectives. This might suggest that the book is closely argued, integrating the advice and information systems perspectives with useful information. We hope that this is true, but in a book designed for use as a reference as much as for a single read through, it makes sense to disentangle the issues to some degree. Thus, Chapters 2 and 4 provide the main theoretical part of the book: Chapter 2 deals with the nature of information systems as a discipline of study, while Chapter 4 considers the research approaches used within the field. These two chapters offer our own distinctive perspective on the field, and should be read in a critical frame of mind. Information systems is a relatively new area of study, and ideas of the scope of the field and appropriate research methods are keenly debated.

Chapters 3 and 5 provide the main 'advice' sections: Chapter 3 considers issues related to choosing a project, and Chapter 5 is concerned with planning and scheduling work. The following four chapters offer more specific information and guidance: Chapter 6 discusses how to survey literature in support of a project, while Chapter 7 is about collecting data in the field. Chapter 8 discusses how to analyse such data, while Chapter 9 examines issues relating to writing up a research report. In the final chapter we summarize our overall approach and outline some of the qualities that examiners look for in good project work.

Taking a research approach

The exact character and scale of the projects that information systems students undertake vary enormously. They may be practical, with a strong hands-on computing element; they may be case studies, surveys or market research; they may be in the form of a consulting assignment addressing a real problem for a real client; or they may be 'pure' studies based on theoretical investigations carried out through careful use of the literature. In this text we speak of all such assignments as research projects. In writing we also use the words 'student' and 'researcher' interchangeably.

Using the word 'research' is not intended to frighten off the nervous or those who feel that their particular skills are of a more practical character. We speak of research projects because we believe that a spirit of research – exploration and discovery – should be at the heart of all students' project work. Something important is to be found out, revealed or discovered, and this task is to be approached in a scholarly fashion. By this we mean in a methodical and self-conscious manner and in such a way as to give rise to new facts or insights that are backed by appropriate evidence. That being the case, research is the right word to use, and people who undertake research are researchers.

One of the most important aspects of taking a research approach is the need for a self-conscious choice of an appropriate process of discovery. To do research requires that this process of discovery, and not just the results of investigations, be set down and communicated. In order to convince their audience, researchers need to describe their methods of investigation and justify why they chose them. The wider community judges and interprets the results of research projects very largely on the basis of the process used and the extent to which it is clearly set out and justified. This process will need to be chosen and justified on the basis of a statement of the aims of the research, the topics to be investigated or sometimes, more formally, the hypotheses to be tested. Once the process is clearly established and justified, then other people can judge the value of research findings and may even be persuaded to act upon them.

Communication of research findings to a wider community will often imply presenting research results in terms of recommendations for action – *how to do things, how to set about solving a particular class of problem* or even *how to proceed in a particular situation*. This form of final output from research is common within the information systems field and derives from the practical concerns of people and organizations that struggle to use information technology effectively. On other occasions, however, research findings may be expressed more in terms of a statement of causality, *how or why things work the way they do*, and it may equally be appropriate at times to offer a more general insight, *how we might think about certain things*, or just *how other people think about these things*. Nor should we forget the value of simply *describing things* as an information system is built, implemented and used. Research that has a strong descriptive element can have enormous value in providing the wider community with valuable food for thought, though achieving such a rich or powerful description is not an easy task at all.

Summary

- Projects are an important part of most courses in information systems. Such project work provides a valuable opportunity for students to test their knowledge and understanding of the field through a substantial piece of work.
- To achieve good results from project work, students need to master a number of research skills and develop the ability to schedule and manage their work.
- Success in projects comes, in part, from choosing areas of study that are of interest to the student and that maintain a clear and identifiable 'information systems' focus.
- The findings of research can be in many different forms, ranging from very specific recommendations for action in one context, through to a broad and persuasive description of how things are perceived or understood.
- Good research that will convince a reader needs to convince in respect of the approaches and methods used, as much as in the findings presented.

Further readings

There are a large number of general books on study skills or undertaking student projects. The Howard and Sharp (2002) book is quite general in its focus, and provides introductory coverage of many aspects of what it is to do research. Bell (1999) is targeted at people undertaking social science projects and educational research in particular, but is nonetheless well worth reading and the advice given is easily generalizable to the information systems context. Dunleavy (1986) should make interesting reading for a student at any time in their academic life; the chapters on writing essays and dissertations are particularly relevant.

Dunleavy's more recent book on PhD research (Dunleavy, 2003) also contains much relevant and useful information, particularly on how to write, and has a potential readership far beyond people actually hard at work on a PhD. Denscombe (2002) provides a sound theoretical grounding in the main tenets of academic research broadly from a sociology perspective. Hart (1998), though ostensibly about just one aspect of doing research, contains many useful contributions and practical tips for working with ideas and concepts. Finally Wisker (2000) gives a more inspirational and motivational account of the research endeavour.

Bell, J. (1999) *Doing Your Research Project: A Guide for First-time Researchers in Education and Social Science* (Milton Keynes: Open University Press).

Denscombe, M. (2002) *Ground Rules for Good Research: A 10 Point Guide for Social Researchers* (Milton Keynes: Open University Press).

Dunleavy, P. (1986) *Studying for a Degree in the Humanities and Social Sciences* (London: Palgrave/Macmillan).

Dunleavy, P. (2003) *Authoring a PhD Thesis: How to Plan, Draft, Write and Finish a Doctoral Dissertation* (London: Palgrave).

Hart, C. (1998) *Doing a Literature Review* (London: Sage).

Howard, K. and J. A. Sharp (2002) *The Management of a Student Research Project* (Aldershot: Gower).

Wisker, G. (2001) *The Postgraduate Research Handbook* (London: Palgrave).

References

Checkland, P. (1981) *Systems Thinking, Systems Practice* (London: Wiley).

2 The subject of information systems

- **What is information systems all about?**
- **Origins of information systems**
- **A maturing field**
- **Information systems today**
- **Still a bit dubious**
- **Addressing technology**
- **Information systems are social systems**

In the past thirty years or so the 'new' academic subject of information systems has appeared. This chapter explores the character of this emerging field, and sets down a tentative account of its shifting domain of study. The chapter tries to offer evidence to support the claim that information systems has truly emerged as an academic discipline, but we also note some qualifications and as a young and dynamic field of study, there is still much to be debated and alternative versions of the essential scope of the field are apparent. It is not, therefore, the intention that this chapter should offer a definitive and complete account of the field. Rather the chapter seeks to identify certain common themes and to highlight particular issues that require further thought and study. While each student in the field must work towards his or her own distinctive understanding of information systems, those undertaking research projects of the type that this book deals with do need to maintain a clear link with the existing body of empirical findings and with established information systems theory and practice. For this reason it is useful to be aware of the origins of the field and its broad outlines, and be able to orient any particular topic of study to the enduring themes found within this discipline.

What is information systems all about?

What is the subject of information systems about? It would be very convenient if we were able to answer the question with a neat and widely accepted definition, and then move on. However we cannot.

There are of course plenty of definitions of information systems available, almost every textbook provides one. For example, the definition of an information system, offered by Davis and Olson (1985) in one of the first comprehensive information systems textbooks, is still fairly representative:

> an integrated, user-machine system for providing information to support operations, management, and decision making functions in an organization. The system utilizes computer hardware and software; manual procedures; models for analysis, planning, control and decision making; and a database.

Avgerou and Cornford (1998), ten years later are less technically oriented, reflecting a broader and more social and organizational focus:

> we can start by using the term to refer to information and data handling activities in human organizations. Information handling in this sense is a purposeful activity sustained over time, and includes the activities of collecting information, storing it, directing it to appropriate places and utilizing it in various tasks within the organization.

Such definitions may be of some use when studying information systems topics for the first time, but they do not help much as one pushes further into the field. In particular, they probably are not of much use when we start to do our own research on information systems. Rather, we need to consider the scope of the field and the history of the subject in order to understand where the study of information systems comes from, how it has developed and changed, and the forces that have shaped it.

Origins of information systems

Information systems is a relatively new field of study, but it certainly has not emerged spontaneously or fully formed. Rather, in order to achieve a distinct identity as a field of study, it has struggled to distinguish itself from a number of other more or less established subjects. It has equally had to develop alongside a set of rapidly developing information technology industries that have come to form a very significant part of the economies of developed countries.

The origins of the academic study of information systems are most directly traced back into the broad area of computer science and the field of information systems has long sought to develop an identity distinct from computer science and software engineering (Friedman and Cornford, 1989). This distinction can be simply (and perhaps contentiously) made by suggesting that, while computer science is about how computers function as hardware and software, and software engineering is about building technical systems – ensembles of hardware and software – that meet given specifications, Information systems is about understanding what is or might be done with these technical systems, how they come to be developed or chosen, and most importantly, their effects or consequences in the world.

This we might loosely call the world of information and communication technology's 'application', though that may be a bit too restrictive if we understand applications in a narrow way and as just about deliberate or rational choices of technology. More generally we can see that such concerns tend to shift the emphasis towards some engagement with issues relating to peoples' interests and attitudes, the nature of organizations and how they work, and the way that society accommodates change. The emphasis is thus moved from engineering concerns and rationalities towards the social sciences.

The relationship between the putative field of information systems and that of computer science has never been an easy one. The desire of computer scientists to establish their scientific credentials has led them to emphasize theoretical and scientific principles based largely on mathematics. This has in turn led to a relative rejection by the computer science community of the study of mere 'applications', and the problems of their development, in favour of the search for a deeper theoretical understanding of computation. For researchers interested in what information technology means in a wider setting – the organization, the workplace, the home or the national or global economy – computer science has had little directly to offer and people interested in such issues have looked elsewhere.

There is, of course, the established field of software engineering that has emerged out of the 'art' of computer programming. This field does sit to some degree between the two concerns outlined above – the computer as an artefact of science and the computer as application and use within a social setting. The core of software engineering is the process of taking a specification and turning it into a software product. Such a specification is generally expressed, at minimum, in terms of functional requirements (what a system is required to do) and a data model (information structures that model relevant aspects of the world within which a system is to operate). In its way, such a specification will express many real world concerns about what is to be achieved, recognises contextual constraints, and identifies who is directly involved; for example, tasks that the computer is to undertake, the environment into which it will fit and the need for interfaces for people involved with and using the technical system. However, software engineering still retains a primary focus on a process to support the production of a high quality technological product, rather than on achieving an organizational effect or promoting change. Furthermore, during a couple of decades of sustained development, software engineering has not substantially expanded its boundaries to include such organizational concerns.

That said, we should acknowledge the increasing emphasis that software engineering has given to such topics as managing software development within projects and as team activities, devising improved means of eliciting requirements and expressing them in a specification, as well as incorporating a sophisticated conception of the human–computer interface into software engineering practice. As software engineers have developed and refined their focus to address these types of topic, they have provided an essential input into the broader field of information systems. But we would argue that software engineering can never encompass the whole range of issues that need to be addressed when information systems are studied in the full richness of their operational and organizational setting.

Thus the second principal point of departure for the study of information systems has been from fields that concern themselves with the study of organizations (as opposed to the study of technology *per se*). Since formal organizations (businesses, government departments and public agencies) have been the primary context for the deployment of information technology over that past fifty or so years, it has seemed appropriate to study information technology directly within such contexts, for example through case studies, and by using (or borrowing) the theoretical and methodological approaches used by other disciplines which study organisations and management activities. This has led the field of information systems to develop a strong concern with issues of how organizations are structured and operate, and where and how new forms of information handling are conceived of, planned and implemented (Scott Morton, 1991; Currie and Gallieis, 1999; Ciborra, 2000). Thus the information systems field has drawn extensively from management science, organization theory, sociology and social psychology. In some areas the relationship has been a two-way one, such that issues raised by the new means of information handling have influenced organizational theorists – see for example, Drucker (1988) or Zuboff and Maxmin (2003).

Another influential factor in understanding the emergence of information systems as a distinct discipline has been how, through the 1990s, information technology and information systems rose to prominence within the field of strategic management. Concepts such as competitive advantage, knowledge work, efficiency and productivity, marketing channels, industry structure and value chains were all seen as having to be reworked and rethought in terms of the significant effects of a burgeoning set of new information technologies and the consequent need for explicit policies of information management (Porter and Millar, 1985; Scott Morton, 1991; Hammer and Champy, 1993; Jones, 1994; Earl, 1996).

Throughout this period more and more businesses and public sector organizations have been encouraged to identify their main information handling activities as 'strategic systems', not just vital to their operations but an important determinant of their success and a strong component of their competitive strategy. One consequence of such shifts in thinking has been that information systems and technology infrastructures have become increasingly self-consciously managed in their own right, becoming the direct concern of senior managers and information systems has become increasingly a discipline that has addressed issues of how information and communication technologies are thought about and applied within organizations, and the effects that they have. This development was in some contrast to the earlier tradition of information systems, addressed almost exclusively at a project or functional level, and concerned with configuring technology to some previously identified or given need, an approach that seldom concerned itself directly or proactively with organizational direction or strategy. Some recent authors even see this debate as coming full circle. An influential article by Nicholas Carr in the *Harvard Business Review* in 2003 was entitled 'IT doesn't matter', and argued that IT had become so standardized and commoditized that it was no longer the basis for strategic advantage, and therefore needed to be managed in a minimal and defensive manner. The new rules for IT management that Carr proposed are certainly provocative to many in the information systems field: spend less; follow don't lead; focus on vulnerabilities not opportunities (Carr, 2003).

Carr's article, of course, had many fierce critics and most people still see building the right information systems, and managing them in the right way, as posing significant challenges that require to be debated within an encompassing frame of reference. Information systems remains a central topic of discussion within senior management circles, and what is done with information technology is usually viewed as of more significance than just efficiently processing transactions or servicing middle managers' information needs through a management information system.

We should also acknowledge that as the field of information systems has developed it has been recognised that computers are no longer the only or even primary technology to be considered. The arrival of new and widely used technologies such as the Internet, World Wide Web, mobile phones, digital television, portable devices and wireless networking all shook up the field in the 1990s and brought with them new media and business models such as MP3 music sharing or the production of open source software. Now it is more often understood that a broad array of contemporary information and communications technologies (ICT) should be acknowledged and understood, and seen as an opportunity or a provocation for radical change, for doing wholly new things in wholly new ways, and perhaps for reshaping or transforming organizations and the industrial and social structures in which they exist. The shift, in Europe at least, from the abbreviation IT to ICT reflects a common recognition of the significance of a range of emerging generic technologies and associated new possibilities for social arrangements, organizational forms and business models.

One recent example of such a shift is shown by the intense interest, commitment and activity that e-commerce has attracted since the end of the 1990s, including the boom and bust of the 'dot.coms' – new companies established to aggressively exploit the opportunity of electronic commerce. Notwithstanding the translation of many dot.coms to dot.bombs, e-commerce has survived and developed more extensive and deeper roots, now seen as a dominant mode of operation in some industries such as air travel, and or potentially revolutionary consequence for others, such as banking or music. The Internet, World Wide Web and experience of e-commerce have also reinforced a new concern for e-government and the transformation of the public sector through ICT (Heeks, 1999).

To encompass such perspectives and such continuing change, and to make the link between diverse technologies under rapid development, the pursuit of organizational innovation and consequential social changes, the field of information systems has had to expand its boundaries beyond narrow issues of current technologies and their management – beyond even the formal business or administrative organization. Significant and influential strands of research in the last decade have pursued a more general understanding of the environment within which information technologies are developed and deployed, both within the fabric of people's lives, and in the organizations and social structures that they participate in (Dutton, 1999). In taking this route the information systems field has often rubbed shoulders with another new discipline the validity of which is often questioned, media studies (Silverstone, 1999). The two fields share many common concerns in understanding the economic and social consequences of new technologies, ranging from concerns with issues of gender, the digital divide and globalization, the future of work, citizenship, education, surveillance and privacy, through to the changing spatial dimensions of a world wired for high bandwidth communications.

A maturing field

Long ago Feldman and March (1981) expressed information systems' mix of technology and social/organizational concerns as being based on a dialectic between students of information behaviour on the one hand and information engineers on the other. Information engineers 'hope to design information systems with some clear elements of sensibility (*sic*) in them'; while for students of behaviour the problem is to 'understand actual human encounters with information'. This notion of a dialectical process (a debate) is often useful in understanding information systems as a field of research, in that it sees contradictions as fruitful collisions of ideas from which a higher truth can be reached. One general aim of research might then be to establish a sufficiently rich view of actual experience with technology so that contradictions can be detected and then explored.

An early example of such research is given by Zuboff (1982), who observed contradictory views of senior managers and line managers concerning some new information systems. The senior managers believed that the systems were put in place to allow more autonomy for line managers, while the line managers saw the systems as a tool for their senior managers to exercise enhanced control. This 'contradiction' can provide a deeper insight into how information systems might be designed and implemented, but it also gives a more general insight into how organizations actually work and the organizational politics that surround information and information systems. Neither version of events was more correct than the other, and both versions were genuinely held by key participants. Simply to study the technology involved, or the declared aims of these systems at the time they were developed, would have allow no resolution of these contradictions, indeed it may not have revealed them at all.

We have suggested above that information systems' areas of concern inevitably draw it towards the social sciences, but the strength of these links is at times tenuous; limited perhaps to a cursory recognition of the organizational context within which technology is deployed. The most potent driving forces within the field of information systems are still, for the most part, derived out of a technical and engineering perspective allied to fairly narrow managerial concerns. This is easy to see in many introductory textbooks, but is equally so if you read more advanced research journals or stop to consider the names that represent the prevalent themes or concerns of the field; for example in the last decade we have dealt with, enterprise resource planning (ERP), office automation, business process re-engineering (BPR) or the ubiquitous use of the word 'system' to describe, as it were, concrete phenomena (e.g. a human resources system, and accounting system). This is matched by a strong emphasis on the pursuit of highly normative instructions as to how to do things, for example in systems development methodologies, with far less emphasis placed on the more subtle questions of choosing what to do and justifying why.

One explanation for this strong normative tradition lies in the basic beliefs and prior experience of many who have come into the field with an essentially technical education. Such an 'engineering' perspective easily translates into an approach that sees organizations themselves as 'machines' that are formal and rational in their procedures and hence provides a suitable environment for technology as a programmed automaton following a defined set of instructions (Walsham, 1991).

An interesting example of this technical focus at work is the recent interest within the information systems development community in object-oriented methods (Krutchen, 1999; Jacobsen, 1999). This interest is quite explicitly based on developments in object-oriented programming, with object-oriented design coming in the middle. The principal force that initiates and drives development in these directions is a technical one – a particular style of programming and software construction. The assumption is made, more or less explicitly, that because object orientation is seen to be a 'good thing' at a technical and programming level, it then follows that an analogous analysis or modelling process needs to be created. This is not to argue that it is necessarily wrong to pursue such avenues; perhaps issues of technology *should* drive analysis methods. Perhaps indeed our technology is so weak and fragile that it demands an analysis process tailored in its image. But if this is so, then it is an expression of a very particular view of the balance of technological to other forces.

Such concerns with finding ways of making technology work for us leads to the third powerful formative influence on the emergence of the information systems discipline; the practical needs of organizations that use ICT. Excellent technology, productive development processes and keen organizational insight, when available and taken individually, do not seem to be enough for modern organizations. They crave for practical guidance as to how to marry these elements in such a way as to derive real benefit; reduced costs, enhanced productivity, a more effective work process and workforce, or a strategic competitive advantage. Such demands have reinforced the information systems discipline's normative flavour, and promoted the development of myriad methodologies, frameworks, checklists and (at times simple-minded) formulae for success, even snake oil.

The influence brought to bear on information systems research and teaching by the needs and aspirations of the largest consumers of information technology, business organizations and government, has been apparent almost since the birth of the computer. An early response was in the establishment of the field of study of management information systems or MIS, emphasizing and prioritizing the role of computers to support managers (see Davis and Everest (1976) for a collection of early writings on MIS). Indeed, in the United States, MIS is still used as the basic description for most introductory information systems teaching and most information systems research and teaching takes place within business schools and for the most part follows their vocational and business driven agenda.

Meanwhile, in Europe, MIS as a taught subject or a research theme gained acceptance more slowly. In part, this may have been because of the relative absence of business schools and MBA teaching thirty years ago. One result was that during the 1980s and into the 1990s, a more technological point of departure was taken in Europe, with issues of practice more likely to be addressed within computer science or computing departments (Avgerou, 2000). Various national and European Union initiatives to promote information technology research on the basis of a 'technology push' model of economic development reinforced this trend through the period. This has led in turn to a deep interest in Europe in information systems development methodologies, both aside from and encompassing software process models (Olle *et al.*, 1991; Avision and Fitzgerald, 2002). Such concern with systems development methodology has allowed the exploration of a number of fields that challenge or contrast with the sharper business and management focus of MIS. Thus, European researchers have explored such areas as participative approaches to systems design, soft systems methods, and problem structuring perspectives (Land and Hirschheim, 1983; Mumford, 1995; Checkland and Scholes, 1990; Rosenhead and Mingers, 2001).

Information systems today

If one broadly accepts the account of the emergence of the information systems discipline discussed earlier, as drawing on both the scientific and engineering traditions of computer science and the social science traditions of management and organizational studies, and adds to this the practical requirements of those who use computers, then one may very easily identify information systems as a multi-disciplinary or hybrid field of study. Indeed, there are many other areas of established knowledge upon which work in information systems draws; for example, psychology for understanding issues of human–computer interaction, economics in determining the business value of a company's investments in information systems or political science in exploring the effect of ICT on government activities and the role of the state.

It has been, however, the conviction of a growing body of specialists that information systems is more than a convenient meeting point for a variety of fields or disciplines that see an *ad hoc* relevance in understanding ICT. Rather, they would claim that the distinct notion of an information system can provide the basis for an explicit and coherent body of scholarship, building up its own theoretical principles, and with a contribution to make which is independent of any contributing fields of study. Swanson and Ramiller (1993) express this in the following terms:

> we are ourselves optimistic that the common bonds of interest in information technology among researchers will prove as durable and lasting as information technology itself appears to be ... Once attracted to the IS academic village, many scholars will continue to choose to reside there, and will carry on the building of a heterogeneous, and yet congenial, community.

We can also offer some empirical evidence to support the contention that this new discipline (or academic village) has indeed emerged. First, there is a coherent body of scholars, sustained over a period of time, which show signs of intellectual vitality and growth. For example, in the United Kingdom there are currently atleast five established academic journals published quarterly which state their principal area of interest as being the field of information systems (*European Journal of Information Systems, International Journal of Information Management, Information Systems Journal, Journal of Strategic Information Systems,* and *Journal of Information Technology*).

In terms of other academic activity, the discipline is now recognized as a distinct field for both textbook publishing and the publishing of scholarly research. A search made in February 2004 of the Amazon on line book store at the American site (Amazon.com) reveals 4358 books listed with 'information systems' in the title, the best seller being Laudon and Laudon's textbook – 18,359 in the best seller ranking:

> Laudon, K C and Laudon, J P (2004) *Management Information Systems: Managing the Digital Firm.* Upper Saddle, New Jersey: Prentice Hall.

Interestingly, the UK site (Amazon.co.uk) does not allow quite the same search to be made, but the first book with the phrase in the title – 3,508 in the best seller list – was shown as:

> Chaffey, D, Bocij, P, Greasley, A and Hickie, S (2002) *Business Information Systems: Technology, Development and Management in the E-business.* London: FT Prentice Hall.

Conference activity, another barometer of the health of an academic field, is at a higher level today than at any time, and one of the oldest major information systems conferences, the *International Conference on Information Systems*, will have its 26th annual meeting in 2005. The *European Conference on Information Systems* is currently (2005) in its thirteenth consecutive year. In 1995 the UK Academy for Information Systems (UKAIS) (www.ukais.org) held its first annual meeting and this has developed as a lively association for UK academics in information systems. Finally, the directory of information systems faculty maintained by the international Association of Information Systems (www.aisnet.org) at www.isfacdir.org lists over 7000 persons in universities and research institutions around the world, all of whom have chosen to be listed.

Perhaps of more relevance to the readers of this book is the emergence of information systems as a subject within the undergraduate and postgraduate programmes of many universities, and increasingly as the title of a distinct department within such institutions. In February 2004 the UCAS website (www.ucas.ac.uk), the standard listing of UK first degrees, showed 1731 undergraduate courses indexed under the word *information*, the majority of which linked it to either *information systems* or *information technology*. The most common index entry (532) was *information systems*, while 332 were entered under *business information technology*. About 80 institutions offer these degrees, often in combination with other subjects. These courses, and the departments offering them, will each have their own distinct character and history. Some have grown out of the computing area, some out of management and business studies, while others are *de novo* attempts to support the new discipline; yet they all choose to use the name 'information systems'.

Still a bit dubious

It should be clear that we (the authors) belong to that group who see information systems as a distinct and necessary subject for study, and an appropriate one to be found in its own right in institutions of higher education. However, not everybody with an interest in the field shares this conviction. For some people, information systems is still but one strand of the discipline of software engineering or computing, while for others it is just a part of business management or even a sub-field of sociology. Yet others, while generally showing goodwill to the idea of a discipline of information systems, worry that coherent theoretical underpinnings are just not apparent, and that there is too much danger in proclaiming a discipline, albeit a potentially useful discipline, without fundamental intellectual support.

In this spirit King (1994) reviews the information systems 'field' from his perspective as the then editor of one of its most prestigious research journals *Information Systems Research*. Note that he uses quote marks around the word field to indicate its still dubious nature. King speaks of information systems as, 'an intellectual convocation that arose from the confluence of interests among individuals from many fields who continue to pledge allegiance to those fields through useful ties of various kinds'. He then goes on to argue for the vital importance of these reference disciplines, both as a means to provide a sound intellectual basis for work, and to provide guidance and orientation when information systems researchers enter new and unexplored territory.

King makes a particular argument for the newness of the territory that the field explores, as well as the currently transient nature of the field. He writes, 'What unites the information systems community is a shared interest in a phenomenal event – the rise and consequences of radical improvement in information technology'. This, he contends (and most in the field would probably agree), leads on to revolutionary change with revolutionary consequences. Such a revolutionary character of the current times is often alluded to by those who work within information systems. Thus, in Cash *et al.* (1994), a modern business school oriented textbook, the authors speak in the preface of a situation in which, 'the tools and concepts that drove the twentieth-century, industrial-era organization are insufficient for managing the information-age organization. Concepts that held up well for much of the century – strategy, structure, span of control, organizational boundaries – are shifting on their foundations. Many of these changes are enabled by information technologies, which managers use to fundamentally alter organizational purpose, shape and practices.' Ciborra, goes further and argues for a crisis and a fundamental loss of control, noting for example, that the Internet has 'emerged as a flexible infrastructure outside any strategic master plan' (Ciborra, 2002).

King, however, notes that revolutions are episodes in history which come to an end. A discipline built in a revolutionary epoch may have little validity once the exceptional becomes absorbed into the everyday, an argument that is similar to the position taken by Carr (2003) and noted above. This should perhaps not be seen as an argument against the existence of information systems as a field of study, and anyway, ten years after King wrote, we still see ICT just as if not more implicated in radical organizational and social change and posing manifest challenges that need research attention. As King said then, 'We are present at an enormous natural experiment that will reveal to the observant fundamental knowledge about ourselves and the world. ... We can learn a great deal from such momentous phenomena if we pay attention and are not distracted from the phenomena by constant demands that we put our disciplinary house in order.' It seems that the experiment continues.

Addressing technology

This brings us to one of the fundamental issues for information systems, the relationship the subject has with technology. We probably assume a strong technological interest at the core of most information systems work, but if we look we may not always find it clearly expressed, and even if or when we do, it will often raise another more fundamental question – how *should* we think about or address technology in our research? Mowshowitz (1981) provides a useful review of underlying approaches and rationalities that are seen applied to technology studies, though writing over twenty years ago he speaks of 'computers' rather than ICT. He suggests the following five perspectives that can be found in the research literature.

- *Technism:* The computer is an instrument of progress.
- *Elitism:* The computer is an instrument of progress but it must be controlled by those with the appropriate skill and insight.
- *Progressive individualism:* The computer is an instrument of progress but we must recognize the imperfections of its actual deployment and work to improve and ameliorate them.
- *Pluralism:* The computer is a neutral technology with benefits and drawbacks for society. It must be made accountable and placed under democratic control.
- *Radical criticism:* The computer is out of control and a threat to human society. We must question the real nature and power of this technology.

In these terms, it is possible to classify broadly most work within information systems and establish its relations to technology. Thus work that directly explores and develops technology falls under the perspective of technism, or more subtly perhaps under the heading of elitism. Indeed the tension between these two perspectives is quite palpable; for example, in the tension between the world of 'cheap and cheerful' PC computing or easy come and easy go web sites (computing for all – free enterprise and laissez-faire), and the more reserved world of a science of software engineering – powerful but obscure with right ways and wrong ways and a strong sense of hierarchy and professionalism. Work taking the socio-technical perspective, discussed further below, would fall most naturally under the heading of pluralism, while most mainstream MIS-focused work is perhaps better classified under the heading of progressive individualism. This then leaves the radical critique. It is hard to offer a single account of this perspective. It is in the manner of a radical critique that it is outside the mainstream. However, writers such as Ellul (1980), Weizenbaum (1984), Roszak (1986) and Angell (2001) each present an analysis that questions the technological imperatives that others seem to accept.

In a recent article Orlikowski and Iacono (2001) return to this question of the relationship that information systems researchers have with their technology, and they suggest that often it is not very strong. They argue 'the field has not deeply engaged with its core subject matter – the information technology artefact' and that 'IS researchers tend to give central theoretical significance to the context' while 'the IT artefact tends to disappear from view, be taken for granted, or is presumed to be unproblematic once built and installed'. They propose a categorization of perspectives on technology found within information systems based on a study of research articles, which identifies five main views of technology that are taken in research:

- *Tool view:* Technology is seen as a means to some end, for example for labour substitution, to increase productivity or to perform some needed information processing.
- *Proxy view:* In this case something else is taken to stand for technology, perhaps human perceptions (attitudes), or number about a technology's diffusion (uptake, spread), or money spent.
- *Ensemble view:* This approach sees technology within some broader network of interests, for example within a development project, in an industry's production networks, or as embedded in some other social system as in studies of virtual communities.
- *Computational view:* This view emphasizes technology as intrinsically a manipulator and processor of data; it focuses on algorithms to support some such activity, or on models that can represent a phenomena of interest.
- *Nominal view:* Finally Orlikowski and Iacono suggest there is the nominal view, a situation in which technology is not really present at all. Some research, they suggest, that claims to be about technology may on closer examination reveal no real substantive concerns. They use the example of some researchers into virtual teams who fundamentally believe that the presence of the technology makes no difference to the thing they are really interested in studying – which is team behaviour.

This critical account has provided a useful challenge to information systems researchers to remember that they are supposed to be interested in technology, and that this requires that they be explicit in exposing the account of technology's significance or role in their work. Orlikowski and Iancono's article is broadly critical of the information systems field, and accuses it of having forgotten its origins and being in danger of loosing its unique claim to relevance. In order to address this issue they suggest the following guiding principals to underpin information systems research and help it to achieve a stronger engagement with technology:

- IT artefacts are not natural, neutral, universal or just given.
- IT artefacts are always embedded in some time, place, discourse and community.
- IT artefacts are usually made up of a multiplicity of often fragile and fragmentary components – and should not be seen as uniform, whole or unified.
- IT artefacts emerge from ongoing social and economic practices, and undergo transition over time.
- IT artefacts are not unchanging, at all times their stability and functioning is conditional and may be challenged.

The discussion here of technology and the approaches to it is not intended to suggest that all information systems research should indulge in anxious navel gazing, trying to locate 'the meaning of life' within otherwise concrete, useful and applied types of research. Rather what is intended to be reflected here is a very practical concern for information systems researchers, how to establish a clearly stated relationship with ICT in their work. This is, after all, one of the primary claims upon which the whole field rests. Given that not all information systems researchers are active shapers of technology, in the sense of systems development or programming, and given the diverse contexts in which information systems studies are found, people working in the field, including student researchers, have to carefully consider how they are implicitly defining technology and thus how they are able to go on to study it.

Information systems are social systems

The discussion above is intended to provide a (relatively) neutral panorama of the information systems terrain. In this section we wish to be more specific, and to express our own perspective. This is particularly important in a book such as this, since the reader needs to know the basis from which the advice and information given is drawn.

Our point of departure is the phrase *information systems are social systems*. This phrase can be traced back at least as far as a paper by Land and Hirschheim (1983) in which they wrote 'an information system is a social system that uses information technology'. Angell and Smithson (1991) take up the theme and write:

Information systems are social systems whose behaviour is heavily influenced by the goals, values and beliefs of individuals and groups, as well as the performance of the technology. As such, the behaviour of information systems is not deterministic and does not fit into any formal algorithmic representation.

This idea, essentially an ensemble view in the terms of Orlikowski and Iancono discussed earlier, goes a long way back into the history of information systems, if one takes it as an expression of the more general socio-technical perspective. This was first given a clear expression in the studies undertaken in coal mines in the 1940s by researchers at the Tavistock Institute in London (Trist and Bamforth, 1951; Emery and Trist, 1960). These studies sought to show that new technology could not be introduced successfully into coal mines simply on the basis of its supposed technical merits. If it was to work, that is to deliver what was understood as its potential, it had to be embedded or situated in an appropriate social system. Those who undertook to introduce the new technology needed to consider this and to work to develop both a particular implementation of the technology and a social situation in which it could work. In the case of the coal miners Trist and Bamforth studied, this suggested less hierarchy and functional division and more team-based methods of working (Ciborra, 1993).

Such socio-technical ideas have explicitly underlain a number of developments in information systems thinking up to the present day; for example, work on participation and in particular Mumford's ETHICS methodology (Mumford, 1995; Land and Hirschheim, 1983). A well argued statement of the socio-technical perspective applied in research is contained in Davis *et al.* (1992) in which an information systems' failure is explored using an interpretive approach and on the basis of exploring technical characteristics *and* social and organizational features. In this context the authors explain the need for adopting such a perspective in that neither an exclusive focus on the social systems nor the technical systems, would satisfactorily explain what actually happened. Indeed, and of direct relevance to the research theme of this book, they suggest that an investigative or analytical perspective that ignores one or the other aspect will in all probability never collect much of the raw data, perhaps will never uncover it. They argue therefore for a focus that is able to encompass and integrate both aspects.

In the past decade the socio-technical perspective has been reinforced by much work that has considered new and flexible technologies such as in computer supported cooperative work (CSCW), knowledge management and all manner of web-based systems. At the same time, for some within information systems the older socio-technical tradition has needed to be reshaped and taken in new directions through a broader move to encompass a perspective that draws more explicitly upon social theory. Thus Avgerou (2002) and Monteiro (2000) both acknowledge the long history of socio-technical ideas, but also suggest that they are currently being transformed by new concerns and new possibilities for understanding technology.

Socio-technical approaches have, nonetheless, for the most part been normative, concerned with establishing a standard. The aim in most cases is to propose a method or to give advice that can be used in such a manner as to result in 'better' systems in use. We must recognize that such approaches are underpinned by a particular set of values held by their proponents. These values then dictate what will be recognized as a 'better' system – be it in terms of job satisfaction, social cohesion, feelings of security or self worth, or acknowledgement of the rights of workers to involvement in the development of the work processes that they are a part of. From here it is also understood (but usually less well specified) that being 'better' in these terms will lead to other organizationally desired benefits. For example, that a contented and fulfilled workforce working with systems that they feel are appropriate to their own needs will in turn provide enhanced levels of service to customers, which will translate into improved profitability. This takes us back to the original work of Trist and Bamforth which was concerned with achieving organizational benefits out of technology (mining more coal) by means of a focus on the human and social dimension.

Within the constraints of the values that it implies (and there are real constraints), the socio-technical approach can thus give some more general pointers as to what a 'better' information system is and how to achieve it. In this sense it is one that works within a given social context, one that is institutionalized and becomes embedded as a substantive part of an organization. Thus there is a stream of research within information systems that is described as *implementation* research, and which looks at the mechanisms and processes that are apparent when a new information system is set to work. This view has taken particular notice of phenomena of resistance to the change implied by new technologies, and the appropriate means to either understand it or to thwart it (Keen, 1981; Walsham, 1993).

More recently, a strong interest has developed in the ways in which information systems can emancipate or empower the individual or the group. This may be seen as making people more productive (effective) by supporting their inherent abilities as information handlers (flexibility, intelligence, decision making) at the same time as serving their needs as human beings (autonomy, control, security, society). Zuboff (1988) describes these aims in terms of a perspective that recognizes two distinct approaches to the use of information technology – the informate/automate divide. 'To informate' is a new verb that she coins to describe a use of information technology in such a way as to augment human effort, to provide more information to 'local' workers and to service their requirement for autonomy and a coherent framework for decision making. When information technology substitutes for human effort it *automates*, when it augments human effort it *informates* (Cash *et al.*, 1994).

What 'information systems are social systems' then means is not just that we must look beyond technology if we are ever to understand what happens when information systems are put to use. Rather it is *only* if we have identified, described and analysed the people, people-structures and people-processes involved, that we can truthfully say that we are taking an information systems perspective, or considering an information systems issue. We must however emphasize again that this is not a position intended to deny technology, far from it. In the words of Orlikowski and Robey (1991, p. 151), we are concerned at the very least to treat technology as an important *social* object, perhaps with fixed material features, but certainly with indeterminate social implications. The use of such technology is then an occasion for change and often a provocation to existing structures.

We can, however, go further than this and argue that ICT, is itself the product of a social process at various levels – a position known as social constructivism. These levels range from the macro level – national research and development policies promoting particular types of technology, through to the micro level – a particular office choosing a particular type of desk-top publishing software. Thus, ultimately, it makes no sense to separate the social from the technological.

Summary

- The field of information systems is a young academic area. The exact dimensions of the field are not always clear, and information systems research will often draw on other more established disciplines. Important contributing areas include computer science, software engineering and business management.
- A healthy academic community has developed around the study of information systems, and increased levels of activity in research, publishing and conferences support this.
- Researchers in this area need to carefully think about and develop their concern with technology, and recognise that engagement with technology can come in many ways and be based on many accounts of technology's significance.
- The socio-technical approach is one substantial intellectual tradition that has sought to resolve these issues and continues to do so.

Web resources

Amazon online books store (UK site) www.amazon.co.uk
Amazon online books store (USA site) www.amazon.com
Association for Information Systems www.aisnet.org
International directory of information systems faculty www.isfacdir.org
United Kingdom Academy of Information Systems www.ukais.org
Universities and Colleges Admissions Service (UK) www.ucas.ac.uk

References

Angell, I. and S. Smithson (1991) *Information Systems Management: Opportunities and Risks* (London: Macmillan Press).

Angell, I. (2001) *The New Barbarian Manifesto: How to Survive the Information Age* (London: Kogan Page).

Avgerou, C. (2000) 'Information systems: what sort of a science is it?', *Omega, International Journal of Management Science*, vol. 28, pp. 567–79.

Avgerou, C. (2002) *Information Systems and Global Diversity* (Oxford: OUP).

Avgerou, C. and T. Cornford (1998) *Developing Information Systems: Concepts, Issues and Practice*, 2nd edn (London: Macmillan Press).

Avison, D. and G. Fitzgerald· (2002) *Information Systems Development: Methodologies, Techniques and Tools*, 3rd edn (Maidenhead: McGraw Hill).

Carr, N. G. (2003) 'IT doesn't matter', *Harvard Business Review*, vol. 81, no. 5, pp. 41–49.

Cash, J. I., R. G. Eccles, N. Nohira, and R. L. Nolan (1994) *Building the Information-Age Organization: Structure, Control and Information Technology* (Homewood, Ill: Irwin).

Checkland, P. and J. Scholes (1990) Soft Systems Methodology in Action (Chichester: Wiley).

Ciborra, C. (1993) *Teams, Markets and Systems: Business Innovation and Information Technology* (Cambridge: Cambridge University Press).

Ciborra, C. (2002) *The Labyrinths of Information: Challenging the Wisdom of Systems* (Oxford: OUP).

Ciborra, C. and Associates (2000) *From Control to Drift: The Dynamics of Corporate Information Infrastructures* (Oxford: OUP).

Currie, W. L. and R. D. Galliers (1999) (eds), *Rethinking Management Information Systems* (Oxford: OUP).

Davis, G. B. and G. C. Everest (eds) (1976) *Readings in Management Information Systems* (New York: McGraw Hill).

Davis, G. B., A. S. Lee, K. R. Nickles, S. Chatterjee, R. Hartung, and Y. Wu (1992) 'Diagnosis of an information systems failure: A framework and interpretive process', *Information and Management*, vol. 23, pp. 293–318.

Davis, G. B. and M. H. Olson (1985) *Management Information Systems: Conceptual Foundations, Structure, and Development* (New York: McGraw-Hill).

Drucker, P. (1988) 'The coming of the new organization', *Harvard Business Review*, vol. 66, no. 1, pp. 45–51.

Dutton, W. H., ed. (1999). *Society on the Line: Information Politics in the Digital Age* (Oxford: OUP).

Earl, M. J. (1996) Information Management: The Organizational Dimension (Oxford: OUP).

Ellul, J. (1980) 'Technique and Non-power', in Woodward, K (ed.), *The Myth of Information: Technology and Post-industrial Culture* (London: Routledge and Kegan Paul).

Emery, F. E. and E. L. Trist (1960) 'Socio-technical systems', in C. W. Churchman and M. Verhulst (eds), *Management Science Models and Techniques*, Vol. 2 (Oxford: Pergamon) pp. 83–97. Reprinted in Emery, F. E. (ed.) (1969) *Systems Thinking* (London: Penguin).

Feldman, M. S. and J. G. March (1981) 'Information in organizations as signals and signs', *Administrative Science Quarterly*, vol. 26, no. 2, pp. 171–86. (Reprinted in Galliers (1987) cited in further readings below.)

Friedman, A. L. and D. Cornford (1989) *Computer Systems Development: History, Organization and Implementation* (Chichester: Wiley).

Hammer, M. and J. Champy (1993) *Reengineering the Corporation: A Manifesto for Business Revolution* (London: Brealey).

Heeks, R. (1999) *Reinventing Government in the Information Age* (New York: Routledge).

Jacobson, I., G. Booch and J. Rumbaugh (1999) *The Unified Software Development Process* (Reading Mass: Addison-Wesley).

Jones, M. (1994) 'Don't emancipate, exaggerate: Rhetoric, reality and reengineering', in R. Baskerville, S. Smithson, O. Ngwenyama, and J. I. DeGross (eds) (1994) *Transforming Organizations with Information Technology* (Amsterdam: North-Holland).

Keen, P. (1981) 'Information systems and organizational change', *Communications of the ACM*, vol. 24, no. 1, pp. 24–33.

King, J. L. (1994) 'Editorial notes' *Information Systems Research*, vol. 4, no. 4, pp. 291–8.

Krutchen, P. (1999) *The Rational Unified Process: An Introduction* (Reading, Mass: Addison Wesley).

Land, F. F. and R. Hirschheim (1983) 'Participative systems design: rationale, tools and techniques', *Journal of Applied Systems Analysis*, vol. 10, pp. 91–07.

Monteiro, E. (2000) 'Actor-Network Theory and Information Infrastructure' In *From Control to Drift*, C. Ciborra (ed.) (Oxford: OUP).

Mowshowitz, A. (1981) 'On approaches to the study of social issues in computing', *Communications of the ACM*, vol. 24, no. 3, pp. 146–55.

Mumford, E. (1995) *Effective Systems Design and Requirements Analysis* (London: Macmillan Press).

Olle, T. W., J. Hagelstein, I. G. McDonald, C. Rolland, H. G. Sol, F. Van Assche and A. Verrijn-Stuart (1991) *Information Systems Methodologies: A Framework for Understanding* (Wokingham: Addison-Wesley).

Orlikowski, W. J. and Iacono, S. (2001) 'Research commentary: desperately seeking the "IT" in IT research – A call to theorize the IT artefact', *Information Systems Research*, vol. 12, no. 2, pp. 121–34.

Orlikowski W. J. and D. Robey (1991) 'Information technology and the structuring of organizations', *Information Systems Research*, vol. 2, no. 2, pp. 143–71.

Porter, M. E. and V. E. Millar (1985) 'How information gives you competitive advantage', *Harvard Business Review*, vol. 63, no. 4, July–August, pp. 149–60.

Rosenhead, J. V. and J. Mingers (2001) *Rational Analysis for a Problematic World Revisited: Problem Structuring Methods for Complexity, Uncertainty and Conflict* (Chichester: Wiley).

Roszak, T. (1986) *The Cult of Information* (Cambridge: Lutterworth Press).

Scott Morton, M. S. (ed.) (1991) *The Corporation of the 1990s: Information Technology and Organizational Transformation* (New York: OUP).

Silverstone, R. (1999) *Why Study the Media?* (Thousand Oaks, CA; London: Sage).

Swanson, E. B. and N. C. Ramiller (1993) 'Information systems research thematics: submissions to a new journal', *Information Systems Research*, vol. 4, no. 4, pp. 299–330.

Trist, E. L. and K. W. Bamforth (1951) 'Some social and psychological consequences of the longwall method of coal-getting', *Human Relations*, vol. 4, pp. 3–38.

Venkatraman, N. (1991) 'IT-induced business reconfiguration', in Scott Morton, M. S. (ed.), *The Corporation of the 1990s: Information Technology and Organizational Transformation* (New York: OUP).

Walsham, G. (1991) 'Organizational metaphors and information systems research', *European Journal of Information Systems*, vol. 1, no. 2, pp. 83–94.

Walsham, G. (1993) *Interpreting Information Systems in Organisations* (London: Wiley).

Weizenbaum, J. (1984) *Computer Power and Human Reason* (London: Penguin).

Zuboff, S. (1982) 'New worlds of computer-mediated work', *Harvard Business Review*, vol. 60, no. 2, pp. 142–52.

Zuboff, S. (1988) *In the Age of the Smart Machine: The Future of Work and Power* (Oxford: Heinemann).

Zuboff, S. and J. Maxmin (2003) *The Support Economy: Why Corporations are Failing Individuals and the Next Episode of Capitalism* (London: Allen Lane).

Choosing a project **3**

- ■ **Considering project options**
- ■ **Selection of study area**
- ■ **A project proposal**
- ■ **Project support**
- ■ **Starting work in earnest**

The previous chapter has presented a fairly abstract account of the origins of information systems as a field of study. Nevertheless, as we will see, many of the issues discussed there do have practical relevance when embarking on a student project. In this chapter we turn to such practicalities and start by considering how to choose a project area and provide some structure to your study.

The first activity to be undertaken before you can start detailed work on your project is to decide on the area in which it will be based, the particular focus of the work (the research question) and the approach to be taken. The purpose of this chapter is to provide some guidance in making these decisions, addressed largely to the problems faced when launching an individual project within the constraints that apply for final year undergraduates and Masters course students. In other words, this chapter is written with a realistic view as to what a student can achieve when limited by time, resources and experience. These limitations are very real and in student projects must, out of necessity, condition the approach taken. For example, under such circumstances a final submission date will almost certainly be set, and resources such as computer access, software and library facilities will also be restricted. Perhaps most important of all, such a student will only have limited experience and knowledge in the chosen area, and will be neither an expert in the topic chosen nor an experienced researcher.

We separate the task of choosing a project into three main phases. The first is the informal thinking stage when vague possibilities are generated, reviewed and (usually) discarded. The second activity is reviewing selected study area(s), and the third is planning or designing a particular project within a chosen area. This three-stage process is intended to help in arriving at a project that is of genuine and sustained interest, is achievable, and will satisfy the examiners for the course in question.

Like much of the good advice we get in life, the ideas and suggestions made in this chapter may be annoyingly prescriptive. It would be nice to do all the things proposed here, and we know we should, but we say: 'time is short', 'I know exactly what I want to do anyway', 'my adviser will make all the decisions', 'I don't have any special interests', or 'what I really want to know is what is the minimum I can get away with'.

If any of these thoughts occur to you, then be very careful. You may be a project disaster waiting to happen, and when it happens you will be solely to blame!

Considering project options

For most students a few minutes reflection on 'what project will I do?' should reveal a large range of interesting themes to work on. The possibilities available may range from a theoretical investigation of some aspect of computing or information systems, to a practical systems development project for an outside client. Other possibilities may present themselves too, a case study of some existing information system, tracing its history and evaluating its strengths and weaknesses, or a study of the management strategies used in a particular organization to plan and develop new information systems.

Chapter 5 contains some more examples of projects, based on work that we have supervised in recent years. Many institutions also keep libraries of past projects, and it may be a good idea to browse there too in order to gain a general impression of the style and focus of projects that other students have undertaken. If you do this you should of course bear in mind that not all projects are good projects, and not all good projects necessarily provide a good blueprint for other students. However, it is reasonable to expect teachers to give general indications as to those past projects that can provide sound models.

It is a good principle that projects should draw on and develop as far as possible some material that is contained in prior information systems or computing courses that a student has taken. Equally, most information systems students, at least at the undergraduate level, will have recently taken courses in other relevant subjects; for example, operational research, management science methods, marketing or accounting. Projects that draw on and consolidate material from such subjects may make very good sense, not least as a tactic to reinforce the subject matter of the 'outside' course. On the other hand, information systems projects should have a clear information systems focus; a project on the implications of information technology for management accounting may be a valid topic, but it will not be successful *as an information systems project* if it is exclusively or even mostly about management accounting.

Projects as opportunities

Your project might also be approached as an opportunity to develop a particular new skill or to gain experience with a new tool or technique. It may be the chance to learn a new programming language, gain experience with a new package, or to develop a system in a new (to the student) area that requires quite intensive study; for example, multimedia systems. A project can also be the opportunity to study and practise a new systems development methodology, or to gain more general skills, such as those of interviewing, questionnaire design or survey processing.

Projects that are too general, or those that just constitute a survey of basic textbooks or are the rewriting of lecture notes will seldom please examiners or achieve high marks. Examiners are usually looking for evidence that you have *done* something, not just read around and summarized a subject using standard literature. This implies an expectation that a student should go out into the world and collect some data, seeking out various sources of information including the literature of information systems, experts in the topic area, experienced practitioners, and people who use and work with information technology. Evidence of such activity is usually expected to be shown in a project report, and may require such elements as summarized accounts of interviews, the results of questionnaire surveys and the questionnaires themselves, or critical descriptions of how particular information systems were developed and operate.

Some students will have arrived at their final project after taking many technical and software-oriented courses. They may as a result feel that the only possibility available to them is to do more of the same. However, within an information systems project there should be at least the possibility to range beyond an application-based or exclusively computer-focused project, and to undertake work that operates on other boundaries of the discipline, for example exploring and utilizing organizational and social perspectives. To undertake a project with such an intention may well be a very valid way of broadening a student's perspective on technology.

This is not to say that practical and hands-on components should not be a part of any project, or that a software development exercise is not an appropriate topic for an information systems project, far from it. As set out in Chapter 2, the field of information systems is a broad church, and encompasses many varied disciplines skills and techniques. This suggests that projects based around software development efforts can very well incorporate and utilize some other relevant themes, for example consideration of aspects of user participation in systems innovation, or work in the area of human–computer interfaces.

If a practical, technology-based, analyse-design-implement type of project is undertaken, it may well be useful to give it an information systems slant even if it is approached in the form of a conventional software engineering project adhering to the mainstream project life-cycle. Within the conventional software process it may be possible to give a stronger focus to some particular aspect in a way that allows the approach to be developed in new directions; for example giving more attention to software testing issues, requirements determination techniques or code reuse. Remember too that a practical information systems project does not necessarily have to result in software. It may equally well focus on the analysis activity required prior to any software design, or the development of an architecture for a system using standard packages and web tools, such as scripting languages, spreadsheets or databases.

When undertaking practical software development projects it is usually good advice to base them on a real requirement with a real client. Projects that are based on hypothetical or general sets of requirements often generate poor and unreal results, since they lack the authenticity that comes from being matched to a real situation and real interested parties (users). That said, there might be certain standard software problems that are discussed in the literature that do possess the potential for revealing a good project topic. For example, building software to play a game of poker or draughts is a recurrent test case for knowledge-based systems, and might offer a good opportunity to review literature in the area and to explore alternative algorithms or architectures.

Whatever the project focus finally chosen, it makes sense to expect that it will be based on some strong information systems themes. In this way you should seek to explain the direct link between the particular work you will undertake or situation studied, and some general questions or debates in the field about how computer-based information systems operate, are developed and are used. The discussion in the previous chapter should help here, allowing you to reflect a little on which aspects of information systems you are principally drawing upon or even seeking to contribute to, and how any potential project you consider relates to the core technology.

The thinking stage can commence as soon as you become aware that you will need to produce a project. In some ways you cannot start too soon to explore the possibilities and to refine your ideas of the type of project you wish to undertake. It is good advice to start generating ideas for a project as early as possible, possibly even before the course proper starts. On the other hand, you will need to be flexible and to take advice. When students are enjoying their taught courses and developing deeper and richer understanding of information systems, they will be developing new perspectives and understandings that may in turn reveal new or different potential topics to pursue within a project.

Even when it is not desirable or possible to start work in earnest until after the official sign-up date for a course, it may be very useful to begin preliminary tasks earlier. An early resolution of the question is especially important if there are particular set-up tasks to be undertaken, such as writing letters to potential collaborators or making special arrangements with a company or other organization, or learning to use particular software.

Selection of study area

If a couple of competing ideas have been identified through the informal stage, they now need to be evaluated and one chosen. The time has now come for a rather more formal approach to refining and evaluating the study area To address the issues that need to be considered in establishing a valid topic it is sensible at this stage to prepare a written assessment, a *Study Area Review*. This is a brief document that sets out the general case for undertaking the project, and evaluates the resources required and available.

It is a good idea to seek the opinions of other people, including your fellow students, as to the suitability of the study area proposed. This does not just mean in discussion with your direct academic adviser. By writing a study area review it should be possible to solicit opinions from various other people, and in this way to work towards testing and refining your ideas and you should expect to undertake one or two revisions of your review before moving on. The key issues one should consider in a Study Area Review is provided in Box 3.1.

We do not provide here any detailed suggestions about what form a study area review document should take. In any case it will probably be no more than two or three pages of text and it may be largely in the form of bullet points and brief statements. However the main issues to address in the review are suggested in the list above and discussed further below. Of course, these issues should have been implicitly considered during the 'informal thinking' stage, but now is the time to consider them explicitly and to write down your current understanding. In choosing possible areas for study, and in writing one or more Study Area Reviews, you need to take into consideration such

---

BOX 3.1

Key issues to consider in a study area review

- Satisfying your own interests
- Is there anything happening?
- Meeting the requirements of the course of study and having an information systems perspective at the core
- Gaining access to organizations and people
- Availability of materials and equipment
- Access to literature
- The techniques and skills you will need to master
- Level of interest of the topic for other people
- Some topics are just not a good idea – too big, too boring, too risky, too dangerous

---

factors but also remember that the list given above is not meant to be exhaustive, but rather to be indicative of the types of considerations that need to be taken into account.

Satisfying your own interests

The project that is finally chosen will need to absorb your attention for a substantial period of time, perhaps six months and maybe longer. It is therefore essential to feel attracted to the topic, and to be able to sustain your interest. Broader areas of interest, perhaps in terms of future career plans or past work experience may be usefully translated into the project theme. For example, a student who has worked in health services management might choose to study the information systems used in hospital management, or a student who has developed a particular interest in organizational analysis from prior study may wish to use this as a basis for a study of some aspect of information systems implementation.

Is there anything happening?

Many students are attracted to information systems, and information technology in particular, by its newness, the excitement of novel ideas, and the potential impact they might have on organizations or society. This is generally laudable but it does not necessarily fit well with the research focus of a well designed project. Normally you can only research the present or the past (i.e. what is happening now and what has happened). The future comprises largely the realms of speculation and astrology. It may well be that a particular technology may have important implications in five or ten years time but this is very hard to research now. Thus, it is sensible to work on something tangible that is happening now, or has happened in the recent past.

The main exception to this time-orientation concerns feasibility studies or their variants. Organizations (including governments) do have to take decisions now concerning the introduction of new technologies or building new systems in the future and we, as researchers, can contribute to this. So, for example, you could investigate the feasibility of introducing an ERP system into a particular company or the introduction of new broadband networks as part of the economic development strategy for a depressed inner city suburb. But in such cases you should focus more on the present drivers and constraints and less on a rose-tinted long distant future. By all means mention the promises but do not treat them as inevitable and 'just around the corner'.

Meeting the requirements of the course of study

Your project will be assessed by examiners and it is wise to know which criteria they use to assess project work. In particular, it is sensible to try to understand the particular perspective that they take on information systems, and the balance that they make between information gathering, analytical skills, creativity and questions of presentation. A project, for example, focusing on software engineering, economics, accounting or organizational analysis alone may not satisfy them, even though elements of these subjects may be essential to pursuing a good information systems project. Students should keep asking themselves, 'Is a concern with information systems at the heart of this project? How can I justify this project as being essentially concerned with issues of information systems?'

Access to organizations and people

A project is an opportunity to go out and gather up-to-date information from the world beyond the university. Our experience of supervising many hundreds of student projects tells us that people outside universities are, in general, very pleased to talk to students, and they can be surprisingly generous in allocating time and supplying information. Some organizations are positively eager to have students undertake work for them, but it is necessary to make the first contacts and to assess whether subsequently you will have enough access and support.

It is also important that a number of different directions for access and contacts are considered. Projects that depend totally on working with one organization or the cooperation of one person are risky. A safer strategy is to work towards developing links with a number of people or organizations who can all, potentially, contribute to your work.

Working with people beyond the university, and with business and other organizations, also implies an important responsibility on students. If time and effort is freely given then a student should equally respond by respecting the concerns and imperatives of these other organizations. You should remember that your behaviour, and the impression that you make, will condition the reception given to the other students who may well follow in your tracks.

Availability of materials and equipment

There is no point in choosing a project area in which there is no possibility of access to the required materials or equipment. On the other hand, you should do your best to locate what is available, and to secure the best access possible. This can be an issue for practical computing projects that may require intensive use of particular software or hardware, for example a scanner or a high quality colour printer.

In choosing a study area it is important to evaluate the general resources available to support work in the chosen area. On this basis it should be possible to make sensible choices as to the particular form of the project. Thus, if there is not a sophisticated knowledge engineering environment available there may be a more modest expert system shell available as open source software, but there is still the question as to whether you university will let you download it and install it in their laboratory?

Access to literature

An important resource for any student undertaking a research project is access to the best library possible. A project that has only minimal references to source materials a decade or more old will in general not be viewed very sympathetically by examiners, particularly if it is in an area in which a good deal has happened more recently.

The availability of electronic library resources now makes it far easier for students to access up-to-date material, for example through the IEEE digital library http://info.computer.org or the ACM portal http://www.acm.org. Most university libraries will have institutional subscriptions to these and other digital resources, but even individual subscriptions at a student rate are possible. That said, it is not all about using the latest literature, and as is mentioned in Chapter 6, some older classic literature may be important to your topic, and if so it should be sought out and used.

The techniques and skills that you will have to master

In considering potential project areas it is important to understand the particular techniques and skills that will need to be mastered in order to complete the work. It may be very exciting to try to develop an object-oriented, neural network based decision support system for investment risk analysis, but can you master neural networks, object-oriented design and programming, and financial risk analysis in the short time available? In any case, by identifying particular skills that will be needed on a project, it will be possible to schedule some time to master them. Even apparently simple skills, such as interviewing, need to be considered and time spent in researching interviewing techniques or practising them will be well spent.

The extent to which it might be of interest to others

Other people will be involved in almost all projects, at the very minimum your academic adviser, and more probably other people who will be a source of information and opinions. To get the best from these people they need to be interested in the work to some degree, and a topic that you find very exciting may not seem at all interesting to them.

One solution to this is to seek out a project that is suggested by some other person or outside organization. This can be very acceptable, but it is necessary to be sure that such a project meets the examiners' requirements. In practice this probably means that the project will need to be adapted in some ways to meet the requirements both of a client and of the examiners (see also the discussion of working with a client in the next section). In any event, even if someone else suggests your project, it must very soon become your own, and you must take the responsibility for bringing it to a successful conclusion. For this reason we, as project supervisors, are often a bit nervous to suggest specific research topics to our students. At the very least they have to understand that just because we think a topic may be appropriate and worthwhile does not mean that we have all the answers as to how to proceed with the research.

As an example, an outside sponsor may suggest a project developing a database to support a marketing manager in recording client contacts and for direct mailing of advertising literature. This sounds a very acceptable starting point for a project at the undergraduate or MSc level, but to meet the examiners' requirements it will probably need to be expanded, for example to consider the decision making behaviour of such managers, their information needs, and the extent to which the proposed system will provide the expected benefits. In order to undertake the project it may be necessary to investigate similar systems that exist, or available software packages to do the job. If it is possible to build the system in the short period of time available, by programming or setting up a package, it would then be sensible to undertake a post-implementation review of the delivered system. All of this would need to be backed up with some evidence of your understanding of the key issues involved in using information systems in customer relationship management (CRM) and draw on the considerable literature in this field. In this way, by the end, you may find that, while the sponsor may be very pleased with the work done, the project as reported to the university should have taken a very specific shape and reflect more research orientation.

Some topics are just not a good idea

You may find that your enthusiastic ideas for a topic start to run into fundamental problems. Perhaps you find it hard to keep hold of the information systems issue at the centre, perhaps you have chosen a topic that is more about speculation and some wonderful future world, perhaps you have found a topic area that is too difficult to do justice too in the time available. Finally, you may have chosen a topic that will lead you (potentially) into real trouble – an experimental investigation of money laundering, international espionage, cyber crime or pornography. If so, please stop and use your common sense. There are plenty of good, safe, solid and still interesting information systems issues with researchable questions. You only need to find one.

A project proposal

So far we have spoken about choosing a study area and suggested writing one or more Study Area Reviews. Once this is done, and the student and adviser agree on a particular study area, it is important to move on to plan the specific project that will be undertaken and the activities that it will require. There is usually only a limited time available to work on a project, and it is important that, as far as possible, a direct path is taken that will result in a completed and coherent body of work within the time available. This means that it is essential to narrow down quite early on from a general study area to a specific project with a clearly understood set of objectives and a specific method or approach to satisfy them.

In doing this it is important to ensure that you are defining a real problem or studying a real issue, and that it is possible to learn enough about it, analyse it properly, and write it up convincingly in the time allowed. The single most common cause of problems with student projects comes from trying to tackle too large, complex or ill-defined topics. If this is combined with an *ad hoc* approach to planning, then disaster is almost inevitably the result.

When a project can be expressed in terms of six or so concrete aims each with associated activities and clear deliverables for inclusion in the final report, then it has probably been narrowed sufficiently. This advice, of achieving up to six concrete aims with associated activities and clear deliverables, is equally applicable to an undergraduate project and to PhD research (though of course the aims themselves may be more ambitious in the latter case!).

The *Project Proposal* that is produced at this time should contain a structured statement of the basis for the study, the area considered and the questions to be researched. From this it leads on to a statement of the aims of the study, the principal activities envisaged and the resulting deliverables. This document should be dated and may then become a part of the final project report, perhaps as the first appendix. If the project objectives are substantially revised as the project progresses, then an explanation of how the revised version was arrived at should also be included.

A checklist for contents of a Project Proposal is provided in Box 3.2.

BOX 3.2

A checklist for contents of a project proposal

- A well thought out project title
- A half page description of the area of study, justifying it as a contribution to understanding information systems
- Two to four research questions that might be the main focus for the project, and an outline of the kind of argument that might be developed
- Identification of parts of the syllabuses of other courses that are relevant
- Five to eight key words or key phrases that you could use to search an online library catalogue
- Description of alternative ways of approaching the topic to gain data. How have other researchers gained their data?

▶

▶

- Assessment of questions of access to the required information? List the other people or organizations that you expect to gain information or help from, including the persons you wish to act as advisers or mentors
- A description of any required skills you need to acquire or IT resources to locate
- Key references to books or journal articles that you see as providing a theoretical context to your work. As a rule of thumb a minimum of five such sources should be sought. In any event, a single source is dangerous, as is reliance on standard textbooks
- What are the critical activities, people or resources that can make or break your project? Where is the risk? What can you do about it?
- Finally, you will need to break down the project into specific aims that you set yourself (up to 6)? You will then need to expand each of these in terms of: the understanding you need to achieve; the activities you need to undertake; the deliverables expected.

Carefully develop your project title

Good projects flow from good project titles: does it frame an interesting or important question; will it attract a reader's interest? It is important that you know from this early stage what it is that you are trying to do, if for no other reason than to enable you to explain to other people and to gain their cooperation in your research, and a clear title is a good way to express this. This is not to say that projects or their titles should be carved in stone and never changed, but it is good discipline to attempt to distil the essence of your work early on.

Some people suggest that a title should be in the form of a question, as for example, *Will Open Source Software Find a Market on the Desktop?* The argument is that by framing the title in this way, the reader is attracted to the work, and the researcher is always clear as to what the outcome of the work should be – that is, some kind of an answer to the question posed. Other people find this question form less helpful, and prefer a descriptive title as for example, *Secondary Schools Use of the Internet to Build Relationships with Parents*.

Titles can be in the form of a transition from the general to the specific (often done with a colon): *Technology for Data Mining: The case of Mobile Phone Marketing*, or *Health Informatics for Developing Countries: A Case Study in India*. They may also be the other way round, from the specific to the general: *The*

Prima Clinic Information System: A Study of Health Informatics in Developing Countries.

A good title tells us something about a project, attracts our attention and gets us ready to read on. An example of a poor title that fails these tests, taken from a real recent project, was: *Evaluating, Developing and Implementing an Information System in an Organization.* The project itself was good and received a quite high mark, but that title hardly sold the project!

Here are some recent project titles based on work of our own students. Consider which ones you think pass the test and are informative and interesting. Which ones would you feel are less successful? Can you improve them?

- Targeting Terminal Terrorism
- Development of a System to Improve the Efficiency of the Back Office Operation of a Boutique Fund Manager
- A System to Control the Workflow For Analytical Laboratories
- Innovative IT and Customer Relations in the Manufacturing Sector
- The Privatisation Phenomena: Do Information Systems Matter?
- Customer Relationship Management Systems Play a Key Role in Organizational Success in the Banking Industry
- Evaluating the Business Value of Internet based E-Commerce for Small and Medium Sized Enterprises in Tropicana
- Is Information Technology Critical to the Success of Mergers and Acquisitions?
- Information Systems and Competitive Advantage
- Internet Usage in Ruritania

Another useful exercise is to read through a few issues of some information systems journals and comment on the quality and appropriateness of the titles used for the research reported there.

Project proposal checklist

The checklist in Box 3.2 above is intended to summarize some of the guidance given in this section and to help you start to produce a Project Proposal. Not every project will have an obvious positive response under each heading, but viable projects will have positive responses under most headings. In any case, a fairly stable version of the answers to these questions should be in place after the first few weeks of work so as to allow you to move on to the next phase.

The next two pages give a pro-forma for such a Project Proposal. It covers the main areas you will need to think through, though different types of project may require rather different types of presentation.

Project proposal form

Author:	Date and Revision number:

Working Title:

Main Theme: (A description of the area)

Research Questions: (Possible questions drawn from the area)

1.

2.

3.

Outline of argument or position: ("In this project I will try to argue that....")

Links to wider Information Systems issues (Potential area to draw on and to make a contribution to)

Links to syllabus of other units within the degree (useful material to draw on)

5 key words or phrases for use in an online search e.g. of the ACM Digital Library

Alternative ways to research the topic and to collect data: (If possible, give examples of other people's work in the area and summarise their approach)

Required resources and issues of access:

Assessment of required skills or techniques:

References to 5 articles or books relevant to the topic and which you have read

Justification of interest to others: ("This topic is of importance and wider interest because …")

You should now attach to this form a statement that breaks down your work into up to 6 separate objectives that you will pursue. In each case there should be a description of the associated activities (what you will do to meet the objective), and the deliverable (outcomes) of this activity.

Example of a project proposal

If the project area has already been established as, say, investigating approaches to knowledge management in government departments, then a simple example of a Project Proposal written up in this form might resemble the following:

Working Title: Knowledge Management in Local Government: Current Practice and Future Potential

Main Theme: Knowledge management ideas seem to have had great influence in many business organizations, and many apparently successful case studies are available. However, in the public sector it seems that far less attention as been paid to this area. This project will look at how far knowledge management ideas have been accepted and operationalized in public administration with a particular focus on local government organizations. The project will also try to gauge how potentially successful they might be based on interviews and/or a questionnaire survey.

Research Questions:

1. To what extent are knowledge management ideas and approaches used in local government organizations?
2. What projects are underway or what actual KM systems are in use?
3. Do these types of organization have knowledge management problems that are the same as, or different from, those found in business organizations?
4. What benefits do government departments expect from knowledge management projects, and are they getting them?

Outline argument: In this project I try to argue that the problems of knowledge management faced by local government organizations are substantially different from those faced by business organizations, and thus it is not surprising that there is less activity in the area and that people have limited expectations of benefits from knowledge management. (Of course the data that I collect may invalidate all or some of these arguments!)

Links to wider IS issues: This study will contribute to the IS field by exploring the idea that different type of organization have different informational needs, and prescriptions that seem to work in one context will not necessarily work in another. In other words, that information systems need to be understood in relation to particular organizational contexts.

Links to syllabus of other units: Management Fundamentals – the nature of managerial and professional work; Introduction to Knowledge Management – standard case studies of KM success, alternative models of how knowledge is captured, codified and disseminated; Advanced Information Systems Management – models of strategic choice for IS managers; aspects of relations between the IS function and broader organization.

5 key words for online search: knowledge management, public sector, local government, systems implementation, e-government

Alternative ways to research the topic: As well as literature reviews I expect to use a mixture of one or more case studies of KM projects in the public sector if possible (I have seen a few of these in journals and magazines), as well as possibly a postal questionnaire to IS managers and some interviews with people working in IS management in local government bodies.

Required resources and issues of access: I have already made contact with the IT manager of the local city council, and with two people who work in the management strategy office of the district council. They have so far helped me to frame the research, and assure me that they can facilitate access for interviews and questionnaires within their own organizations and perhaps with others. They have also pointed me to the main journals, organizations and web sites used within the local government IS community, and in which KM is quite hotly debated. The main resource I foresee as a need from the college is a good digital voice recorder for interviews, and software to process surveys if I choose to use this approach. SPSS – one such package – is available in the computer lab but it seems quite difficult to learn.

Assessment of required skills or techniques: I know almost nothing about statistics or how to design a questionnaire survey. I think I am quite a good interviewer, but I would like to find some training resources to make me even better.

References to 5 articles or books relevant to the topic: (We have not added these here because this is an edited account of an actual project proposal and the references that were cited would now be a bit out of date. Nevertheless, given the courses that had been attended, shown above, and the help given to the student by people working in local government, there was plenty of choice available.)

Justification of interest to others: This topic is of importance and wider interest to others because of the increasing emphasis given to computerizing the public sector and to achieving e-government. Often this is expressed in simple terms of providing web based access to current services but beyond such fairly simple ambitions lays a more substantial project, to make government more responsive, smarter and more effective. To achieve such an aim implies using and sharing more knowledge or knowledgeable practices in the operations of government, but can this happen, and if so how?

As suggested above, there is now a need to start to break down the project into some sub-tasks. We have called these *objectives* here, because they represent things you are going to try to do in a general way. For each objective we have also suggested some *activities* that you will need to undertake to achieve the broad objective, as well as some *deliverables* or outputs that you will expect to produce from these activities. Later on this information can be the basis for setting out a more detailed timetable with a more concrete breakdown and careful consideration of when each activity is done (see Chapter 5). For the moment, however, the level of detail shown below is about right and stops you from getting in a situation where you are not seeing the wood for the trees.

The attached set of objectives for the project given above might then be presented as follows:

Objective 1. To survey and review knowledge management practices and the various strategic approaches that are taken in organizations.

> *Activities:* Read practitioner literature on knowledge management (KM). Survey last two years of management journals for knowledge management articles (using specialist online database). Use an online search to find articles and reports on KM in the public sector from quality newspapers and magazines and from specialist conferences etc.
>
> *Deliverable:* Review of KM and its application in the public sector – about 2000 words.

Objective 2. To understand the key theoretical perspectives on knowledge used in the KM field, and how these might affect the way KM is proposed and pursued in different organizations.

> *Activities:* For the most part, literature based research, following up leads from textbooks and journal articles. Use library online catalogue to check what is available. Write up.
>
> *Deliverable:* An annotated bibliography on KM literature – aim for approximately thirty references.

Objective 3. To understand the strategic ambitions that drive KM in local government and the inhibitors that hold it back.

> *Activity:* Arrange 1 or 2 informal interviews with consultants in two management consultancies who work on KM and with public sector clients (initial contact already made as described above). Analyse in terms of (1) strategic ambitions for KM, and (2) key inhibitors for KM. Use as basis for a more detailed study of one (or two) projects, and/or by a survey or set of semi-structured interview (see Objective 4 below).
>
> *Deliverable:* An empirically validated account of key KM issues as seen by people who work in local government – about 2000 words.

Objective 4. To collect case study material from one (and perhaps two) organizations' experience with a KM project.

> *Activities:* Locate organizations and prime contacts (already have contacts who have agreed to help in general). Prepare preliminary letter stating what this project is about. Send to contacts, follow up and schedule interviews. Expect one-hour interviews between two and four persons per organization. Prepare text for semi-structured interviews. Undertake interviews. Write up interviews. Follow up any questions or queries. Write up, possibly each case on its own, possibly on the basis of main issues detected across the different cases – defer decision on this.

> *Deliverable:* Transcripts of interviews for further analysis (an abstract of this could be included in an appendix of the final report but certainly edited down, together with contact letter and semi-structured interview script); Summary of findings from each case study – about 1500 words.

Objective 5. To develop an account of KM that addresses the main issues uncovered in the empirical portion of this project. To make a contribution to the KM literature! To prepare an implementation checklist for use by managers of future KM projects. To make a contribution to KM practice!

> *Activities:* Check on prior implementation models and checklists. Develop my own views of KM and discuss it with those who have contributed to my research. Write up my findings as the final section of my report.

> *Deliverable:* Final section for report – max 2000 words.

We have here broken the project down into five main objectives, each with activities and deliverables. However, we have not linked all the deliverables to specific parts of the project report. Sometimes you will need to do things but they will not directly result in a section for your report. Note also that Objectives 1 and 2 are distinct. One is facing practice, the other theory. Both are needed, but we do not want to confuse them at this point.

Prepare a timetable or schedule of work

On the basis of the kind of planning work described here you should start to get quite a detailed picture of what you project work will be, the things you have to do, and how long you can allocate to each part. On this basis you can start to prepare a project timetable. You will then be able to monitor your progress throughout the period of the project. Within this timetable you will need to allow time for preliminary research, developing skills, making contacts, detailed fact gathering, preparation of the various elements of the project report, production of a full draft report, revisions and final packaging. This aspect is so important that we devote Chapter 5 to it.

Project support

Individual projects

An individual project is the work of one student, but it is not expected to be undertaken completely unaided. Any student researcher needs advice and guidance from a variety of people who have the expertise and experience that he or she lacks. Students are unlikely to be working in an area where nobody has ventured before and, although it is a general requirement of project work to make a distinctive contribution, it is important to beware of 'reinventing the wheel'. Before a project starts it is wise to spend some time identifying those who may be useful to support and add insight to the work. During the duration of a project it is important to pay careful attention to maintaining these relationships, as often a few key words of advice can save many days of fruitless effort.

The academic adviser will usually be the main source of advice and support, but in this section other people who can provide particular guidance are suggested.

The adviser

The exact nature of the help and supervision that is available to students varies. Students work in a wide variety of institutional settings and this means that they have varied opportunities for support and supervision when undertaking projects.

Students who study within a formal college environment can expect to have a direct adviser or supervisor who is intended to be the principal source of advice and support. Even if you do not study within such an environment, you would be well advised to make the best efforts you can to find somebody who can act as a mentor for your work, and who can provide you with vital feedback. Such a person will probably be an experienced information systems or computing professional, but anybody with knowledge of academic projects or research assignments should be able to provide help. It is perhaps unrealistic to expect such a person to become highly involved in the detail of your work, but you should try to get them to undertake two main tasks:

- To assess your project proposal in the early stages, to determine whether it is achievable in the time available, whether it is coherent and complete, and whether it relates to the field of information systems in an appropriate way.
- To review the later drafts of elements of your project report, and to make suggestions for improvements in the presentation of the results.

Students should take advantage of the supervision that is available and arrange to meet with their adviser or mentor regularly. It is most useful to agree on a timetable with intermediate deadlines when work such as outlines, preliminary drafts, data or preliminary analyses are to be presented. Remember, your adviser's or mentor's job is not to chase missing students and it is the student who must take the responsibility for arranging and attending meetings. You alone are responsible for developing your project, and you should do your best to meet and discuss progress with your adviser regularly.

Meetings between students and advisers are most productive when there is a concrete agenda of topics to be discussed. In the early stages of a project this agenda may of necessity be dictated by the adviser, but as soon as possible it should be for the student to draw up the agenda. Indeed, it may be a very good idea for a student to actually draw it up on paper, and to pass it to the adviser in advance of a meeting.

Advisers may be willing to review some drafts of project chapters as they are written but, before submitting a draft, you should check the formatting, spelling and grammar so that the adviser can concentrate upon the content. Some advisors will limit their reading, for example some may only agree to read any part of your project once. For drafts, use double line spacing, to allow the adviser room to insert comments. You must remember that your adviser probably has many other calls on his or her time, and you must be able to fit into their busy schedule. For example, you may have to wait some days before your adviser can give you an appointment and you will have to give them time to read drafts. It is usually sensible to pass them the draft and arrange an appointment to discuss it one week or so later, at their convenience, rather than arranging an appointment just to hand them the draft.

Remember too that advisers are human; they take holidays, they become ill and supervision of your work is not usually their main priority.

Projects for a client

You may decide to undertake a project that analyses or solves a real problem for a real organization. This is certainly encouraged in most institutions and in some it is a requirement. If this is the case you will have a client, the person or organization for which you are working. The client is of course most interested in getting their job done, not in your project report. Even more than with a traditional adviser, a client is typically under external pressures that may mean sudden changes to your support environment. For example, you may be working in an area in which the client has some interest and can provide a high level of support, but this support may be reduced drastically if the resources are suddenly needed elsewhere. In some cases, rather than withdrawing support, the client may feel that they have to press ahead with their work at a faster pace than is convenient for your timetable. In such cases, you will need to try to negotiate a new arrangement with the client that is still mutually beneficial.

To satisfy a client you will need to produce perhaps slightly different outputs than are needed to satisfy the requirements of your course. As long as you are aware of this, it should pose no particular problem. The wordprocessor is helpful in such cases; it is easy to reformulate texts by switching blocks of text around, changing the layout and adding or deleting some material. However, beware that, while this solves some of the low-level problems, it does nothing for resolving any fundamental conflict of interests that might occur between you, your institution and the client. Nevertheless, an acceptable (to the examiners) report may well be possible based around a set of deliverables to a client, with a linking commentary and broader analysis and findings provided by you to satisfy the academic requirements of the project.

Remember too that most examiners are looking for some sense of perspective as to the successes and failures within a project, and this may well require the writing of a separate section in which such reflections are expressed. Examiners may in addition require some further detail on methods and techniques used, detail that you would not choose to present to a client, and this might need to be added too.

Experts in particular aspects of the project

Neither your adviser nor a client will be completely familiar or up-to-date with every aspect of a project, and it is not their job to carry out research on a student's behalf! Therefore, other experts will almost certainly need to be approached, but first they will need to be identified. Your adviser may be able to suggest relevant people and perhaps arrange an introduction. However, if the adviser is not available, you should not waste your time just waiting. Depending upon the nature of the problem, it may be relevant to contact another academic or practitioner (perhaps someone who has published in the area), or a trade association or similar body. A useful source of information can be the specialist groups of professional and academic bodies. Both the British Computer Society and the Operational Research Society in the UK, for example, have a number of special interest groups, and the Chairperson or Secretary of an appropriate group may be able to provide some guidance.

Starting work in earnest

The suggestions made in this chapter are intended to bring you to the point of starting work in earnest on your project. If all the aspects of preparing for research that are outlined here have been considered, then the chances are that the project itself is going to be a success. The time spent in thinking, and in preparing written proposals, will not have been wasted. Indeed, the time spent in preparation is going to save both time and efforts at later stages. With a solid project proposal in place you can feel confident that the project itself will proceed smoothly.

We do however have one final word of warning based on our experience. Students undertaking projects do need to remember that, despite all the help and encouragement that a client, your adviser, a mentor or your boy or girlfriend may give you, this is going to be your project.

You alone must take responsibility for the work and for the final presentation.

Summary

- Start to think about possible project topics as early as you can, but keep an open mind.
- When you have a few solid ideas, take the time to write a brief Study Area Review for each topic. Use this document to stimulate ideas from other people.
- Once a particular area is selected, move on to prepare a full Project Proposal. This should include a clear breakdown of the project in terms of objectives, activities and deliverables.
- Take the advice and support that is available to you, but remember, you must retain the responsibility for your own project.

Further reading

Bell (1999) and Howard and Sharp (2002) cover a number of the topics addressed in this chapter, and Bell has a useful section on negotiating access to organizations for research purposes. Both Hart (1998) and Denscombe (2002) provide useful ideas about what good research is about, and how to set up a suitable project.

Bell, J. (1999) *Doing your Research Project: A Guide for First-time Researchers in Education and Social Science* (Milton Keynes: Open University Press).

Denscombe, M. (2002) *Ground Rules for Good Research: A 10 Point Guide for Social Researchers* (Milton Keynes: Open University Press).

Hart, C. (1998) *Doing a Literature Review* (London: Sage).

Howard, K. and J.A. Sharp (2002) *The Management of a Student Research Project* (Aldershot: Gower).

Web resources

IEEE Digital Library http://info.computer.org

ACM portal http://www.acm.org

Research approaches

- ■ **Problems of research**
- ■ **Positivism and beyond**
- ■ **Ontology and epistemology**
- ■ **Approaches to research**
- ■ **Choosing research approach**
- ■ **Guidance through the methodological maze**

While the previous chapter has provided guidance about how to get a research project off the ground, and the general kinds of issues that need to be considered along the way, this chapter steps back a little and reviews the variety of research perspectives and approaches that are used within the field of information systems. Just like Chapter 2, this discussion is intended to help a student-researcher. In this case to help them select or refine the appropriate research strategy for their own work with a sound theoretical basis. The discussion in this chapter should also help students to understand the limitations of any particular approach that they use, and thereby allow them to offer a more carefully judged interpretation of what they achieve within their project work.

In Chapter 2 the argument was put forward that information systems is a discipline of the social sciences, and that 'information systems are social systems'. Following this line of argument, what follows in this chapter is very much concerned with ideas of approach and method based on recent debates within the social sciences. For those people who have a stronger technical standpoint some of this may seem to be inappropriate for informing their research work. We would however suggest that in the general spirit of this book, all readers should give the ideas discussed here an opportunity to influence them. At the very least they might confirm, and perhaps give a name to, prior strongly held notions of what it is to do research.

Problems of research

In an ideal and simple world it would perhaps be the case that a research project starts from the identification of some issues or questions that just *demand* a process of structured enquiry. From there, research would move smoothly on to the selection of an appropriate research strategy with consequent activities for collecting and analysing data. Finally, the results of research would be so clear cut and obvious as to make their presentation a simple matter of recording what was observed and drawing the obvious conclusions. In Chapter 1 research was described in such general and perhaps naive terms when we wrote:

> Something important is to be found out, revealed or discovered, and this task is to be approached in a scholarly fashion. By this we mean in a methodical and self-conscious manner and in such a way as to give rise to new facts or insights that are backed by appropriate evidence. ... a research approach requires that both the process of discovery and the results of investigations be set down and communicated in an appropriate manner and in such a way that they can be shared with the wider community of interested parties.

These phrases may be good enough as far as they go, but they immediately suggest four aspects for further investigation.

- Where does that 'something' that is to be found out, revealed or discovered come from, and what makes it important?
- What does a scholarly, self-conscious and methodical manner imply?
- How are new facts or insights going to be achieved and how are they judged to be valid?
- What is the appropriate manner in which such facts or insights can be communicated?

These questions have occupied the minds of scientists and philosophers since at least the times of the ancient Greeks, and there are very firm ideas of the correct answers to each of them. These answers, which can be found in the literature on the philosophy of science, address the questions in various integrative ways. However, for a start let us consider each question in turn.

Where do research ideas originate?

In a narrow, day-to-day sense this question is often treated very casually; we investigate what interests us or what we are asked or told to investigate. However, as we discuss below, a deeper analysis of this issue can reveal a lot about our view of the world, as researchers, as well as influencing what type of research approach we adopt. Often we follow current themes and fashions. For example, in 2004 numerous people are researching into enterprise resource planning (ERP) implementations, perhaps for no better reason than that it is a current and fashionable topic. ERP certainly represents a set of ideas that are taken seriously and are being enthusiastically applied in the business world. This may lead to money being made available for such research or to a student determining that a knowledge of this area will improve his or her job prospects.

All researchers are swept along to some degree in the tide of fashion, and it is very hard to stand aside from the interests and concerns of one's colleagues and to pursue odd topics that others believe are of no value. It may also be that, in the short history of information systems, it has been particularly valuable for researchers to stick together for company, with many people at any one time working on similar themes and topics.

There have been attempts to map out a broad research agenda for the discipline of information systems; see, for example, Mason and Mitroff (1973), Ives et al. (1980), Keen (1991) and Avgerou (2000). Keen and Avgerou both note the diversity and fragmented nature of the discipline. While Keen pleads for a more coherent and cumulative research programme for information systems, Avgerou finds efforts to discipline and control the field to be futile. Hirschheim and Klein (2003) advocate the development of a common 'body of knowledge' for the field. These discussions may provide useful insight and can help the student-researcher to find fruitful research avenues to explore. Such frameworks can also provide helpful starting points from which to evaluate and judge prior research efforts.

The rapid development of the technological component of the field may also suggest another reason why, at any particular moment in time, information systems research is bunched around a few key concepts. As new technologies are developed, they demand research attention if only to evaluate their real utility. This was perhaps true of expert systems, local area networks and electronic data interchange (EDI) in the 1980s, and may today be true of such technologies as peer-to-peer networks, open source development and mobile commerce. Thus, information systems research may often take the form of 'constructive' research (discussed further later), in the sense that the research is aimed in various ways at preparing for a new way of doing things with new technologies. In this sense our definition of research extends beyond a study of what *is* and becomes a part of a process of development of *what may be*. However, the novice researcher should take care not to indulge in idle speculation or the repackaging of industry produced hyperbole. It is legitimate to interview a variety of relevant people concerning the application of brand new technologies but students should not be surprised when the promoters of the technologies claim that they will 'change the world'. This is a standard case of the *well, they would say that, wouldn't they* phenomenon.

What is it to be scholarly?

This question is equally often treated in a fairly casual manner. What is scholarly is what we see acknowledged scholars doing. The influence of respected authorities, the contents of academic journals, and the prejudices and opinions of our teachers all tell us quite directly what will be judged as scholarly. A community sharing a consensus as to what constitutes scholarly work in the sciences is what Kuhn (1960) referred to as a scientific paradigm. He proposed a theory of science which sees eras of a stable paradigm, relatively unquestioning and based on widely accepted theories, punctuated by periods of revolutionary change as new ideas gain authority and sweep away the old (or perhaps new researchers supplant the old). These revolutionary periods are then followed by a new orthodoxy – a shift in the paradigm. One example of such a paradigm shift within a long established field of science is the relatively recent shift in the paradigm of geology that has come with the acceptance of the theory of plate tectonics. We should note, however, that while the theory of plate tectonics has only been almost universally accepted in the past three decades, the first expression of the idea of continents fitting together as a jigsaw is at least three hundred and fifty years old, and is often attributed to the English philosopher Francis Bacon.

Kuhn's ideas of scientific paradigms seem to many to have a certain validity within the natural sciences, but have provoked a good deal more debate within the social sciences where it is more common to think in terms of a variety of competing sets of underlying assumptions (multiple paradigms). Indeed the very word paradigm has, we feel, been used so casually that is has become devalued almost to the point of becoming meaningless; in this chapter we try to avoid its use.

As we discuss below, there are fierce controversies within academic disciplines as to what is legitimate practice, and what is illegitimate or valueless. This is often reduced to a question of the merits and disadvantages of particular ways of doing research; for example experiments versus statistical surveys versus in depth case studies. Such debates are for the most part rather sterile and pointless, and to really address this question we need first to look at the next question, since it is out of a notion of what makes a research finding valid that we can develop a notion of what a scholarly research process should contain.

What constitutes valid knowledge?

The question of what is valid knowledge brings us to some fundamental issues that cannot be skirted easily. In order to undertake research we do need to know what a 'good result' would look like, if and when we achieve it. In part, this is a case of starting with an important or interesting research question and, in part, it is a question of doing the right things along the way. However, taking care of both of these aspects cannot ensure that what is achieved has any wider validity or relevance and is appreciated by other people.

Many people within the information systems domain have a scientific or engineering background and will have been educated to have a relatively well-formed and 'hard' notion of what constitutes a valid finding from a scientific enquiry. Most will be familiar with statistical methods and significance testing, the idea of an experiment with controls, or mathematical and logical modelling. They probably also have a notion of science as a subject that develops general theories of universal applicability and that works on a basis of proposing and in some way testing such theories. This framework of thought is generally referred to as positivism, and is discussed further later in this chapter.

However, as noted in Chapter 2, information systems borrows from fields of social science as much as it does from natural science and engineering, and within social sciences the debate as to what constitutes a valid finding from research, and the methods to be used in pursuit of a valid finding, is rather more vibrant. Disciplines such as sociology are divided (more or less) into distinct schools of thought with distinct conceptions as to the nature of the social phenomena that they study, the status and role of a researcher, and the characteristic of valid knowledge. Positivism is strongly represented in the social sciences, but alternative perspectives on research have academic currency and legitimacy too. This matters a great deal for the field of information systems for if or when it utilizes and builds on social science, it must of necessity be aware of the currents of intellectual debate in that field, and position itself accordingly.

How to communicate research?

This final question brings us back to what seems an everyday concern. If we do research but nobody notices, then it is a pretty poor show. This is not just a question of presenting clearly written work in an understandable format; though that may be a hard enough task for the student researcher. Nor is it about the status and standing of the researcher as an acknowledged and respected expert; though that is important too, not least because it has direct influence on careers and incomes. More subtly, the way that research is presented also conveys some of the values and intentions that it embodies apart from the explicit material reported.

With most research endeavours, data (in a broad sense) needs to be collected, some analysis applied and the results presented. But this is not to say that presentation and analysis are isolated one from the other. Good presentation is analytical in the way that a scatter diagram of two dimensional data (say customer satisfaction against weeks of staff training) can show the absence or existence of a relationship. An alternative display, perhaps expressing weeks of staff training on a logarithmic scale, may offer further insight.

Choice of displays is then inextricably linked to modes of analysis, but it does not stop there. Research needs to be presented in such a manner that both its internal validity and its external value are expressed. To achieve the former it is necessary that the research questions addressed are set out and then translated and related to some research process or activities. The result that follows may be at the same time both highly specific and highly opaque. Great detail may be given and sophisticated analytical techniques be used, but the result may be that only the most knowledgeable reader can interpret what the real result is.

Such internal validity should not in general be the sole aim of research. What is needed beyond internal validity is the establishment of a connection between what is done and a wider view of the world. Only in this way can research provide meaning to a wider community. It is too easy to pick up academic journals in information systems and find work reported that signally fails to pass this test – the work is done, and perhaps done well in the sense of a technique suitable deployed, but what the work means or how (or whom) it helps, what it contributes, is never expressed, or is expressed in a banal or blinkered manner. This debate, known as rigour versus relevance, often appears in the information systems literature; Benbasat and Zmud's (1999) article on this theme in *MIS Quarterly* is accompanied by comments from various other authors.

Positivism and beyond

The general question of how we undertake research within the discipline of information systems is a topic that has often exercised the minds of those who work within the domain (Mumford *et al.*, 1985; Nissen *et al.*, 1991; Orlikowski and Baroudi, 1991; Galliers, 1992; Remenyi & Williams, 1996; Galliers, 1997). As alluded to above, there are strong and distinct schools of scientific belief to which most researchers belong and to which, equally importantly, their audience belongs, and the field of information systems is no less influenced in this way.

Exploration of conceptions of how researchers proceed generally start from a discussion of the position of positivism. Positivists believe that all true knowledge we may obtain is based on the observation or experience of real phenomena in an objective and real world. Accepting this, positivist research aims to give rise to objective facts that cannot be disputed. More particularly, the facts produced are seen to have no social values encoded in them and are timeless. Such facts can go beyond the expression of individual observations (e.g. 30% of transactions were handled on the day they arrived) and can express observed regularity and search out causal relationships – in other words propose or validate theories.

Consider the finding that staff with two or more weeks of training achieved a 70 per cent completion rate for transactions on the day that they arrived, and staff without training achieved only a 20 per cent completion rate within a day. These observations from a research study might then be used to validate a general hypothesis that training leads to improved service, and the acceptance of the hypothesis can be backed up with suitable statistics. The hypothesis itself was perhaps drawn from a theoretical position that knowing what you are doing improves performance, and the observations then provide support for the theory.

Of course, this still leaves a question of who received training and how they were chosen. It certainly does not *prove* that training increases ability to perform. We should also perhaps note that, in statistical terms, we are more likely to reject the null hypothesis that there is no relationship between training and performance, rather than to accept the hypothesis that there is (see Chapter 8).

Positivism is an approach that directly reflects the methods of (natural) science and a belief in their generality for all spheres of enquiry. It may further be argued that if these qualities cannot be observed in a particular domain, then there is no opportunity for the practice of any 'scientific method of enquiry'. Some people even reject the very notion of any social science or a science of people's collective behaviour.

There are within the social sciences alternative schools which reject or qualify (to a greater or lesser degree) some or all of the above fundamental tenets of positivism. It is usual, after Burrell and Morgan (1979), to refer to the position of these schools in general by the phrase anti-positivism, though the implication of conflict and denial in the word 'anti' is perhaps unhelpful.

An anti-positivist position is one that cannot accept the clear distinction between facts and values, and rather sees them as intertwined. Some schools of thought develop this argument on the basis of ideological positions; all knowledge, including scientific knowledge, is socially constructed and is therefore conditioned by the values of the society that gives rise to them. All scientific facts, it is argued, are value laden. Others base their position on the more general observation that facts and values are mixed up, and probably cannot ever be wholly separated.

At heart positivism is a position that proposes a particular manner of obtaining knowledge (facts) about the world. There is also the intertwined problem, alluded to the above, of determining the character of the world we explore as researchers: theories of reality. At one extreme there is a view of a single 'real world' that we all share, and from which common observations can be made. This position we may call realism. At the other extreme we may speak of a position of relativism, which holds that there is no reality, just the constructions in individual human minds. These minds are shaped in various ways by human cultures and societies and the language that they use to communicate. This leads on to a position that proposes that beliefs and principles can only have validity relative to the age in which, or the social group or individual by which, they are held. Any 'finding' or new fact that this approach may give rise to is clearly at variance with what would popularly be understood as the status of a (positivistic) scientific (e.g. general, timeless or value free) fact.

The main 'anti-positivism' school found in information systems is that of interpretivism (Walsham, 1993), which is based firmly on the notion that reality is socially constructed and research becomes more a case of trying to understand this construction and how it came about, rather than generating 'facts'. It is normally focused in a particular context (a specific organization or industry) such that the results are not immediately generalizable across other contexts. However, the notion that local organizational cultures, traditions and practices are important to understanding human behaviour is an attractive proposition that can provide general insight. Research in information systems that follows this tradition has grown considerably over the last decade (Walsham, 1995; Klein and Myers, 1999).

Another anti-positivist school of research that is beginning to gain ground within information systems is that of critical research (Ngwenyama and Lee, 1997). This suggests that today's society is based on certain deep-seated structural faults that need to be exposed. This fits with ideologies such as feminism and Marxism and is based on the philosophical positions of writers like Foucault and Habermas. The ability to take such a philosophical position is clearly influenced by the researcher's own ideology and view of the world. We would normally advise young researchers without a strong philosophical background in this area to steer clear of this approach.

What we cannot dispute is that positivism, or more generally the methods of science, work. Through their application our society has achieved tremendous advances over the past three centuries in understanding and helping us shape the physical world, and it is not surprising that such an approach should heavily influence other areas of human enquiry. Indeed it has, but important challenges to positivism have come from those who have directly concerned themselves with the study of human behaviour and human structures, in particular from within the discipline of sociology. This has been expressed in a centuries old debate as to the appropriateness of the methods of science when human concerns and behaviour are the subject of study.

Ontology and epistemology

It is conventional to summarize and structure debates on research approaches around the twin concepts of ontology and epistemology (Burrell and Morgan, 1979; Archer, 1988; Hirschheim and Klein, 1989).

Ontology refers to the underlying assumptions made about phenomena under study – theories of reality. The range of perspectives can be described in terms of a continuum from nominalism – things are what we each individually think that they are (sometimes referred to as idealism) – to realism – belief in an objective reality, a real world – things really exist with real concrete characteristics. The words used to describe this continuum may change; thus Orlikowski and Robey (1991) speak of contrasting positions that see social reality as either objective or subjective – based on the sociological schools of Emile Durkheim and Max Weber respectively. In any event, in between extreme positions there is more or less scope for accepting a degree of intersubjectivity; that is, people can negotiate and agree on *some* aspects of a real world, but must agree to disagree over others. Thus we may agree to agree on the concept of weight (measured in grams), but never agree on the concept of beauty (measured in milliHelens – the amount of beauty required to launch exactly one ship).

Epistemology refers to the type of (valid) knowledge that can be obtained about a phenomenon under study. Burrell and Morgan's continuum for epistemology runs from positivism to anti-positivism – that is, from a position that sees general explanations based on regularity and causal relationships, to one that only gives validity to the viewpoint of the participant within a given activity. Interpretivists thus reject the status of a researcher as a neutral observer and emphasize human interpretation and understanding as a part of valid knowledge (Hirschheim, 1985).

Within the social sciences there is an increasing realisation that the debate between the positivists and the anti-positivists, the realists and the nominalists, is too narrow or sterile, or at the very least inadequate to address the problems of researchers in today's world (see e.g. Orlikowski and Robey 1991). Some speak of a post-positivist era (Hirschheim, 1985), while others explore these issues under the banner of post-modernism (Jones, 1991). Post-modernism is particularly associated with methodological plurality, playing games and the 'death of the grand narrative'. Post-modernism celebrates paradox and the ephemeral, questions the neutrality of the 'rational' (see Ciborra, 1994), as well as explores the multiple signs and meanings that phenomena can induce. As Jones notes, post-modernism finds a hugely enticing challenge when it meets the highly focused and serious (we might almost say pompous) rationality of the computer.

Deetz (1996), building on the work of Burrell and Morgan (1979) argues that research (especially the source of research ideas) can be understood in terms of four discourses: the normative (similar to positivist), interpretive, critical and dialogic, where dialogic refers to a fragmented, local, post-modern discourse.

While we cannot identify a single, late twentieth century movement in social science, and certainly not from within that world, the debate today does seem to be more prepared to countenance plurality and multiple approaches, and allow for variety both in belief and in the methods of acquiring new knowledge. This may be seen as a movement towards maturity and confidence, and within which differences can be discussed and credit given where it is due. Alternatively, it might be seen as a reaction to the poor results that have flowed from a century or more of self-conscious social science, and a sense of the need to restart with an era of what Kuhn would describe as 'pre-science'.

Quantitative and qualitative perspectives

Another currently debated perspective on research in the social sciences is the divide between quantitative and qualitative research. Quantitative research relies on developing metrics (numbers) that can be used to describe phenomena (objects and relationships) under study. Such data can subsequently be analysed using the techniques of statistical analysis. (Natural) science has strongly influenced the widespread adoption of such approaches in the social sciences in general, and in information systems in particular. It may at times almost seem the case that any valid research that seeks to describe situations and outcomes has to follow this quantitative approach. By valid we mean here research that can be published in respected journals. Orlikowski and Baroudi (1991) found that 96.8 per cent of research in leading information systems journals followed the positivist tradition (note the precision of the figure), leaving a very small percentage for those taking a more interpretivist or critical approach. During the 1990s the dominance of positivism lessened and anyway, with any such statistics, much depends how 'leading information systems journals' are selected.

The last decade saw a strong movement for qualitative research methods developing across the whole field of the social sciences, and information systems has felt this influence (Walsham, 1995). Qualitative methods can loosely be defined as those which eschew metrication and seek other means of capturing and analysing (understanding) data. Miles and Huberman (1994) describe qualitative research as usually based on words rather than numbers (though they do allow pictures or video images too). As they express it:

> Words, especially organized into incidents or stories, have a concrete, vivid, meaningful flavour that often proves far more convincing to a reader – another researcher, a policymaker, a practitioner – than pages of summarized numbers.

But it is by no means easy to provide that 'meaningful flavour'. It generally implies that the researcher must spend substantial time 'in the field', collecting unstructured and 'real time' observations, and then work hard to make some sense of them. Observations may, for example, be in the form of interviews, transcripts of conversations or field notes made at the time, but such materials alone do not provide a research result. They must be processed, reviewed, analysed, coded, displayed or structured in some way. Yet even then, the researcher's role and actions are somehow more central and intrusive than in, say, a classical survey based approach with statistical analysis.

Strong advocates of the qualitative approach do not detect any problem here. Indeed, as Archer (1988) states it:

> they reject the idea of generalizability, not just statistical but also analytical, in matters of human behaviour, except in the very weak sense that insights into human behaviour may be generalizable by analogy. According to this view, one should not distinguish the way in which research reports can be 'true' from that in which great works of fiction can be said to show the truth.

Qualitative research is naturally strongly associated with an interpretivist and relativist position, and one that hesitates to adopt the 'scientific' model of a generalizable, objective product from the research endeavour. In this way, it is probably wrong to make the distinction between quantitative and qualitative research simply on the use of or absence of numbers. There are after all words in all research, and some numbers in many 'qualitative' studies.

The real distinction is both more subtle and more substantial. In part, it certainly should be understood as reflecting the 'traditional' split between the positivist and anti-positivist epistemological traditions. That is, qualitative researchers are less certain as to the possibility of the pursuit of a value-free, time and place independent, fact. There is also a strong ontological dimension, in that the qualitative researcher, in seeking out the individual's experience and awarding it its own value, must accept a more subjective view of reality.

Archer (1988), in his extensive review of the qualitative research approach, suggests that within this broad heading one may find three distinct rationales presented. First, there is a position that sees qualitative research as complementary to a quantitative approach and providing access to research questions that otherwise might not be accessible. The second position sees qualitative research as a precursor and poor relation, providing an entry point into new fields of study that may subsequently be treated by 'hard' approaches. In this way qualitative research provides reconnaissance and orientation before the main research effort.

Archer's analysis also identifies a third position, one which sees qualitative research as the only true approach, and a significant improvement on the 'pseudo-science' practised by those who adhere to quantitative approaches (and by implication to positivism). As he proposes it, this view may be based on a notion of social science being in an immature or pre-science stage in which 'empirical research cannot go beyond a "sort of [natural] history", conducted in a disciplined fashion'. Nevertheless, it is argued, one day it may, and the fundamental nature of knowledge about social phenomena is not different from the nature of knowledge in the natural sciences (an epistemological position that does not drive one too far from positivism). This view is contrasted with the more strongly anti-positivist notion that social phenomena are inherently different, and inappropriate for study using (quantitative) methods drawn from the natural sciences.

There is further debate over the role of theory and the appropriateness of 'methods' within the qualitative research tradition. Some see the whole point of qualitative research – getting close to the phenomena under study, participating in and observing a human discourse, learning as one proceeds, telling a 'rich' story – as suggesting that prior method or even prior theory, is not required. One just does it and inductively produces a theory or explanation by the end. Not all qualitative researchers would accept this denial of method, and for example Miles and Huberman (1994) offer a powerful argument in favour of both the use of prior theory to set up and bound a qualitative research project, and explicit methods to be used within a project. Some such methods, including 'grounded theory', and related debates are discussed further in Chapter 8.

Approaches to research

The above discussion may be interesting, but it does not perhaps directly help student researchers in determining how to set about their task. The more pragmatic question to be addressed is the choice of an appropriate approach or method in the context of a particular research topic to be investigated.

The overall research endeavour in information systems, as in any other discipline, involves many different styles and types of work. Loosely, we may speak of a stream of 'theoretical' research and one of 'empirical' research. Theoretical research is concerned with developing and refining a body of abstract understanding of phenomena and issues. It may be undertaken through a purely mental set of procedures, though these will no doubt need to be fed with stimuli from outside sources.

Empirical research on the other hand is work that concerns itself more centrally with observing events in the world (though perhaps in a laboratory setting), and then seeking to 'make sense' of what is observed. Bulmer (1982) gives one slightly jaundiced view of empirical social research when he states that, 'Good empirical research is meticulous in its procedures, precise in measurements, careful in the extent to which generalizations are made from the cases studied to a larger population – and frequently boring and even trivial in its contents'. The last comment is a particularly apt warning for students undertaking information systems research projects.

Naturally the two streams, of theoretical and empirical research, interact. Theory gives motivation to empirical research; that is, it conditions and directs what is observed. Empirical research, in turn, provides evidence to drive processes of theory development. It is also the case that, while empirical research can at times be guided by quite specific rules and methods for procedure, for example, double blind experiments, statistical analysis or interview protocols, the exact details of how theories are made are less obvious and more speculative. Just occasionally empirical data may scream out a theory, in the sense of a vivid relationship, but more often it whispers and some cognitive leap is required to make the generalization (positivism) or to achieve the understanding (interpretivism).

It is fairly easy to list and define different research approaches. We use the word *approach* rather than *method*, as in Galliers (1992), in order to distinguish the idea of an overall (but pragmatic) perspective on the task, rather than just a choice of a particular technique. Indeed in the section on *Choosing research approaches* below we give a fairly conventional listing. However, it is perhaps better to start with a more general description of what a research endeavour might set out to achieve. One such framework is given in Iivari (1991).

BOX 4.1

Three broad styles of research

1. Constructive research methods

   conceptual development
   technical development

2. Nomothetic research methods

   formal-mathematical analysis
   experiments (laboratory and field)
   field studies and surveys

3. Idiographic research methods

   case studies
   action research

He suggests three distinct conceptions of the research task, as shown in Box 4.1 above.

Constructive research

Constructive researchers are concerned with developing frameworks, refining concepts or pursuing technical developments. As Iivari states it, the concern is with 'models and frameworks which do not describe any existing reality, but rather help to create a new one, and which do not necessarily have any "physical" realization (e.g. IS development methodologies)'. In the information systems context there is a vast literature of this nature, and some opportunities to develop such work further. However, new researchers should be wary of the 'bathtub' phenomenon where bizarre associations between concepts or odd bits of data come to mind and they are tempted to shout 'Eureka!' Similarly, those considering constructing new frameworks should realise that information systems is a fairly mature discipline and a new framework needs to contribute something of value to an often already crowded cupboard of frameworks. In a very few cases student-researchers are able to create, modify or refute theories or frameworks, usually based on importing their previous experience and knowledge from other fields (e.g. economics, law). However, for most students, spending months in a library is not going to result in theoretical leaps. Instead, most students are recommended to carry out some form of empirical research based on observation of things that are happening. Assuming that they can do this competently, their contribution is data-led but with an adequate theoretical base, their contribution can rarely be disputed.

Nomothetic research

Nomothetic research is concerned with exploring empirical data in order to test hypotheses of a general character about phenomena studied. Nomothetic research is concerned with a search for (and evidence to support) general laws or theories that will cover a whole class of cases. Such research emphasizes systematic protocols and hypothesis testing within the scientific tradition. Thus in each of Iivari's sub-groups under this heading the impetus is to collect data and undertake analysis in such a manner as to provide general insight: for example, by designing an experiment in such a way as to simulate a range of conditions found in multiple locations in the world. Equally, a survey attempts to achieve generality through careful attention to sampling.

Idiographic research

In contrast, idiographic research is concerned with exploring particular cases or events and providing the richest picture of what transpires. The aim is to understand a phenomenon in its own, particular, context. Idiographic research emphasizes the analysis of subjective accounts based on participation or close association with everyday events. In general, social sciences such as history and geography may be seen as having a stronger tradition in idiographic research, while economics would have a stronger tradition in nomothetic research – since the search is for the general laws of economic systems. Within information systems there is a growing tradition of case studies which might be seen as examples of idiographic research.

Choosing a research approach

Vogel and Wetherbe (1984) provide a classic taxonomy of styles of research within information systems as shown in Box 4.2. This has been used many times as the basis of writings about information systems research and to analyse the published research output from the field. Galliers (1991) provides a development of this summary of research approaches, structured in terms of two broad streams of work which he classifies as the scientific (positivist) and

---

BOX 4.2

Classic taxonomy of research approaches

Case studies
Field experiments
Field studies
Laboratory experiments
Conceptual studies
Reviews and tutorials

Table 4.1 Information Systems research approaches in the context of the scientific and interpretivist philosophies (Galliers, 1991)

Scientific	Interpretivist
Laboratory experiments	Subjective/argumentative
Field experiments	Reviews
Surveys	Action research
Case studies	Descriptive/interpretive
Theorem proof	Futures research
Forecasting	Role/game playing
Simulation	

the interpretivist (see Table 4.1). Research approaches, in his terminology, is the chosen term to describe the general style of a research endeavour, while a method is the application of a set of distinct techniques. The same method (e.g. a questionnaire or statistical hypothesis testing) may be used within very different approaches (e.g. a case study or futures research).

Galliers describes the scientific approach as one that is based on the broader fundamental tenets of positivism, that is, repeatability, reductionism and refutability. The assumption is that the things studied can be described and observed in an objective manner, and from those observations general results can be derived. In a classic scientific approach, the precise observations that are chosen to be made are determined on the basis of some prior theory that is to be tested. In particular, they are chosen in order to offer potential for a refutation of a theory (Popper, 1959). Indeed, Popperian analysis would argue that if it is not possible to provide a plausible possibility of refutation, then there is no scientific research process worthy of the name. This position is seen in the classical statistical technique of hypothesis testing, when a null hypothesis of 'no association between factors' is tested to a suitably low level of significance – typically with a probability of 0.05 (Baroudi and Orlikowski, 1989).

Such statistical techniques also introduce the concepts of type I and type II errors. A type I error is the case where a null hypothesis is incorrectly rejected (a relationship is found where none exists) and is guarded against by the significance level of the test used, while a type II error is the case where a null hypothesis is incorrectly accepted (a relationship is not found where one does exist). In this sense scientific theories can be tested, but all a test or experiment can achieve is to offer evidence to refute the theory (null hypothesis). It is important to remember that a test or experiment in this way can never *prove* a theory true.

Galliers's second broad class, that of interpretive approaches, sees the world of information systems as something that can only be 'interpreted', never fully specified or reduced to theories. More particularly, since information systems include people, there is the variability and psychological opaqueness of the human mind and human intention to contend with. For interpretive researchers, social science, not natural science, is the immediate reference discipline.

One particular issue that has been debated extensively is the legitimacy and usefulness of combining different approaches and methods (also known as pluralism). Mingers (2001) argues strongly for using a combination of positivist and interpretivist methods as they provide different information about the world, while Lee (1991) offers a framework for such integration. We would suggest that such an approach may be suitable for large, multi-researcher projects but we would normally not advocate it for individual novice researchers. This is not to say that you should not carry out a (well designed) survey, followed by some (well designed) interviews but you must have a good reason for this strategy. It should not be mere dilettantism. Each method and approach brings with it a certain overhead in terms of understanding and competence. In the limited time available, and with your limited resources, it is usually better to do one thing well, rather than two things badly.

We do not have the space in this chapter to explore all the styles of research that Galliers includes in his framework. Rather we have chosen to highlight here six approaches that we judge to be particularly relevant to the novice researcher for whom this book is written. The chosen approaches are: laboratory experiments, surveys, reviews, action research and the twin themes of case studies and descriptive/interpretive research.

Laboratory experiments

A laboratory experiment implies a research activity that is undertaken within controlled conditions. Within an experimental research design, the researcher manipulates some variables, and observes the results. Thus there are independent variables that the researcher can control, and dependent variables that are measured. An experiment needs to be carefully constructed so as to expose some issue of interest and to generate appropriate data for subsequent analysis. Most often this data will be quantitative in nature, and will relate to a limited number of phenomena. In the Popperian view, an experiment should be designed to provide some refutation to a conjecture. In this way an experiment that 'fails' (does not refute the conjecture) may be just what the researcher wants.

The restricted laboratory setting for an experiment will suggest that the context is not equivalent to that found in 'real life'. However, this may not always be a major concern. If we undertake an experiment to compare text based and icon based user interfaces, and we use a sample of undergraduate students as test subjects and ask them to search a library catalogue using different software, we may feel quite confident that the findings of the experiment will generalize to a whole class of user interfaces for diverse groups of users. In this way the research findings may (or may not) be applicable to situations of managers reviewing financial data, or aircraft pilots interacting with electronic cockpit displays. At the very least, we need to justify any such generalization from an artificial laboratory situation to the real world, especially when the subjects and the context are very different. For a robust defence of experiments within information systems, and their place in the research repertoire, see Jarvenpaa (1988).

Surveys

A single survey provides a cross-sectional picture of affairs at a point in time. The basic technique may be extended to provide longitudinal data by repeating the process over time. Surveys are usually based on some form of questionnaire but they may also be based around structured interviews. If interviews are used, then they need to be structured carefully, since the power of a survey comes from the same questions being asked in the same ways to each respondent.

Careful attention to sampling can make surveys increasingly representative of their target population. However, to achieve such statistical validity may require far more respondents than an individual researcher can process. More commonly, the researcher has to acknowledge that, while a small scale survey can provide interesting information from a real population, it is not statistically representative. Surveys, if well planned and executed, can generate good quality data about current practices and opinions. However, the survey approach seldom enables a researcher to explore causal relationships directly.

Rather, the survey is the starting point for further analysis and model building. Some practical aspects of undertaking surveys are discussed further in Chapter 7.

Reviews

One way to describe research in this category is to suggest that it looks backwards rather than forwards. That is, the researcher is concerned with charting the development of a set of ideas, and with placing them within a descriptive framework. Most research projects do this to some degree, in the form of an introductory literature review that notes prior work and the current state of knowledge. However, providing such a review may quite legitimately be the principal objective of a research project and for some topics reviews may be the best principal method. Reviews are often used in areas of science, such as medical research, as a way to summarise and 'add up' the results of multiple other studies. A good review can be a very powerful and persuasive form of research and be very influential on thinking within the broader community. As an example form information systems, research into national information technology policy within a particular country is likely to depend upon a review of a number primary and secondary sources, perhaps supported by a few interviews.

A well executed review of prior work can make its own research contribution by providing a more refined understanding of the theoretical and empirical work that has been done in a particular area. Note that Galliers places reviews in the interpretivist category, though that is not how a medical researcher would see them. A good review-style project will have a strong feeling of personal insight, through the selection of items included, and the framework of analysis used to present them. The quality of reviews is not measured just in the number of references and sources cited, and those selecting this type of research need to spend as much effort on refining their framework of presentation, as on exhaustively combing the literature. Remember, a review must contribute something and must answer a valid research question. It should not just be a library catalogue of research in a particular area.

Case studies

A case study is an in-depth exploration of one situation. Thus a case study project might address the implementation of a new accounting system in a particular organization or that organization's development of information systems strategy over a period of time. For most case studies the dimension of time is very important in developing understanding. Cross-sectional snap-shots of a particular situation at one moment in time cannot provide much insight into dynamic processes of change. However, for student researchers reading this book, following a particular situation as it unfolds over months and years will probably not be possible. The time dimension of a case study can however be simulated to some degree by historical research, tracing events back in time.

The great strength of the case study is in the richness of data that can be obtained by multiple means when researchers restrict themselves to a single sit-uation. This leads some people to recommend the case study approach for top-ics and areas of study which are novel or which have little theory as yet. The case study, in this way, might be seen as a preliminary research exercise out of which potential theories can be developed for subsequent validation through other methods. Benbasat *et al.* (1987) suggest end-user computing in the late 1970s as an example of a novel area of computer use, that required case study research to begin to understand the phenomenon. This article also provides a good general introduction to issues associated with establishing case study based research.

Limitations of the case study approach include the lack of control of indi-vidual variables and the difficulty of locating causality. If a researcher identifies with the scientific tradition, then the generalizability of findings from a single case study must also be an issue. In part this can be solved by seeing a world of multiple case studies that develop stronger and stronger evidence for a partic-ular set of relationships. Following this theme, case study researchers will need to locate and use other such studies in order to support their research findings; see Lee (1989) where he proposes a 'scientific methodology' for case studies.

Alternatively, a case study may be seen as an essentially interpretivist approach, and in Galliers's framework it is matched against another category labelled as 'descriptive/interpretive'. Indeed, there is much debate as to where different types of case study belong – Cavaye (1996) provides a good discus-sion of this issue. Walsham (1993) argues strongly for the research potential of 'interpretivist case studies' as a means to develop deeper understanding of information systems phenomena. Walsham is also unconcerned with the problem of generalizability of case study research. He argues that 'the validity of an extrapolation from an individual case or cases depends not on the rep-resentativeness of such cases in a statistical sense, but on the plausibility and cogency of the logical reasoning used in describing the results from the cases, and in drawing conclusions from them.'

A particular type of case study that emphasizes the primacy of the context is the ethnographic study (Rosen, 1991), hailing originally from the field of social anthropology. This involves a deep study of the culture and context of the problem situation. Within anthropology there is some dispute regarding whether the researcher necessarily needs to develop an empathy with the research subjects, perhaps by staying in the context for a long period of time, or whether it is more insightful to identify and analyse 'symbolic forms', such as institutions and behaviours, in order to produce a 'thick description' (Geertz, 1973). Good examples of the application of ethnography in information systems include Suchman (1987), Zuboff (1988) and Orlikowski (1991). We would however warn students that ethnographic studies are particularly demanding in terms of time, effort and the insight needed to produce good work.

Action research

Action research, also known as collaborative research, is an approach where the researcher forsakes their traditional role as observer of events and takes part with the subjects in the problem situation. In the words of Benbasat *et al*. (1987) 'the original intent is to conduct research while effecting change'. For example, a researcher may work with the development team on a systems project, carrying out analysis, design, programming or testing. The research output comes through two parallel processes. First, the researcher uses their theoretical knowledge to shape the activity they participate in; second, through their reflection on this experience, they can relate events to prior theoretical knowledge. Action research is often appropriate when a researcher has a specific skill or insight to offer, and can secure the collaboration of people within the research site to put those ideas into action.

The action research approach has the advantage of bringing the researcher close to a research topic within a real world situation. They are thus able to see it through the eyes of other participants as they participate in work activities (Checkland, 1981). This would normally improve the researcher's insight and understanding of the technical, organizational and social pressures that others feel. Avison *et al*. (1999) argue that using action research, the researcher can focus more on what their subjects actually *do*, rather than what they *say they do*. The danger is that the researcher becomes too closely involved and identified with the research situation, so much so that their focus becomes too narrow and they lose the wider picture which is more easily available to a relatively disinterested observer. Strategies to overcome these problems are proposed by Baskerville and Wood-Harper (1996).

Guidance through the methodological maze

This chapter has covered a great deal of ground and many of the ideas it introduces will require further reading and reflection. The main point that we have attempted to make is that researchers need to reflect on their fundamental beliefs as to the nature of the phenomena that they investigate and the means by which they can generate understanding of those phenomena. Reflection on such topics is not an idle or self-indulgent activity, but one that is very central to good quality research in any field. Within the domain of information systems it is particularly important because of the multidisciplinary character of the field and the conflicting traditions that are apparent.

To address the practical concerns of student researchers, the framework of Galliers discussed earlier provides a solid basis for thinking about alternative styles of research. It suggests first a choice between scientific or interpretivist studies. Within each of these broad themes it offers clear models of specific research approaches, based on particular types of data collection and analysis activities, and particular roles for the researcher.

This is not to suggest that researchers are obliged to locate themselves at a single point within this framework, and to be constrained thereafter to only certain types of activity. Rather the framework is there to be used to refine researchers' thinking and to generate alternative ideas for the style of research that will be undertaken. Galliers in particular suggests that, given a particular area of interest, it is useful to categorize prior research as to its approach, and perhaps to use this as an invitation to 'try something different'.

Summary

- Undertaking a project within a research approach requires that students consider carefully the intellectual basis for their work.
- The influence of the scientific tradition on what we consider as research is strong, but within this field there is a rich set of countervailing ideas that can be used.
- In particular, qualitative and interpretative research perspectives can provide theoretically strong points of departure for research.
- On a more pragmatic level, there are well developed models of particular research approaches that can provide solid guidance to student researchers.
- Researchers need to be self-conscious of what they are doing (the research question), how they are doing it (the approach and method) and why they are doing it this way (as opposed to another way) – there is nearly always an alternative approach or method.

Further reading

For students who have little background in the social sciences it is problematic to suggest where they should start to explore this area. One useful place may be with introductory undergraduate texts in sociology, such as Giddens (1986). An alternative might be to dip into a selection of readings such as Worsley (1991) from where many pointers and points of departure can be taken. McNeill (2004) provides a very easy introduction to sociological research methods with a very practical orientation. The classic reference on case studies is Yin (2002), broadly within the positivist tradition.

Giddens, A. (1986) *Sociology: A Brief but Critical Introduction* (London: Macmillan).
McNeill, P. and S. Chapman (2004) *Research Methods* (London: Routledge).
Worsley, P. (ed.) (1991) *The New Modern Sociology Readings* (London: Penguin).
Yin, R. K. (2002) *Case Study Research: Design and Methods* (Newbury Park, CA: Sage).

References

Archer, S. (1988) 'Qualitative research and the epistemological problems of the management disciplines', in (ed.), A. Petigrew *Competitiveness and the Management Process* (Oxford: Blackwell).

Avgerou, C. (2000) 'Information systems: What sort of science is it?', *Omega*, vol. 28, pp. 567–9.

Avison, D., F. Lau, M. Myers and P. A. Neilsen (1999) 'Action research', *Communications of the ACM*, vol. 42, no. 1, pp. 94–97.

Baroudi, J. and W. J. Orlikowski (1989) 'The problem of statistical power in MIS research', *MIS Quarterly*, vol. 13, no. 1, pp. 87–106.

Baskerville, R. L. and A. T. Wood-Harper (1996) 'A critical perspective on action research as a method for information systems research', *Journal of Information Technology*, vol. 11, pp. 235–46.

Benbasat, I., D. K. Goldstein, and M. Mead (1987) 'The case research strategy in studies of information systems', *MIS Quarterly*, vol. 11, no. 3, pp. 369–86.

Benbasat, I. and R. W. Zmud (1999) 'Empirical research in information systems: The practice of relevance', *MIS Quarterly*, vol. 23, no. 1, pp. 3–16.

Bulmer, M. (1982) *The Uses of Social Research* (London: George Allen and Unwin).

Burrell, G. and G. Morgan (1979) *Sociological Paradigms and Organisational Analysis* (London: Heinemann).

Cavaye, A. L. M. (1996) 'Case study research: A multi-faceted research approach for IS', *Information Systems Journal*, vol. 6, pp. 227–42.

Checkland, P. (1981) *Systems Thinking, Systems Practice* (Chichester: Wiley).

Ciborra, C. (1994) 'The grassroots of IT and strategy', in Ciborra C. and Jelassi T. (eds), *Strategic Information Systems: A European Perspective* (Chichester: Wiley).

Deetz, S. (1996) 'Describing differences in approaches to organization science: Rethinking Burrell and Morgan and their legacy', *Organization Science*, vol. 7, no. 2, pp. 191–207.

Galliers, R. D. (1991) 'Choosing appropriate information systems research methods', in Nissen, H-E, H. K. Klein, and R. A. Hirschheim (eds), *Information Systems Research: Contemporary Approaches and Emergent Traditions* (Amsterdam: North Holland) Reprinted in Galliers 1992 below.

Galliers, R. D. (ed.) (1992) *Information Systems Research: Issues, Methods and Practical Guidelines* (Oxford: Blackwell).

Galliers, R. D. (1997) 'Reflections on information systems research: Twelve points of debate', in Mingers J. and Stowell F. (eds.) *Information Systems Research: An Emerging Discipline* (London: McGraw Hill), pp. 141–57.

Geertz, C. (1973) *The Interpretation of Cultures* (New York: Basic Books).

Hirschheim, R. A. (1985) 'Information systems epistemology: An historical perspective', in Mumford, E., R. A. Hirschheim, G. Fitzgerald and A. T. Wood-Harper (1985). Reprinted in Galliers (1992).

Hirschheim, R. A. and H. K. Klein (1989) 'Four paradigms of information systems development', *Communications of the ACM*, vol. 32, no. 10, pp. 1199–216.

Hirschheim, R. A. and H. K. Klein (2003) 'Crisis in the IS field? A critical reflection on the state of the discipline', *Journal of the Association for Information Systems*, vol. 4, no. 5, pp. 237–93.

Iivari, J. (1991) 'A paradigmatic analysis of contemporary schools of IS development', *European Journal of Information Systems*, vol. 1 no. 4, pp. 249–72.

Ives, B., S. Hamilton and G. B. Davis (1980) 'A framework for research in computer based management information systems', *Management Science*, vol. 26, no. 9, pp. 910–34.

Jarvenpaa, S. L. (1988) 'Technical correspondence: The importance of laboratory experimentation in IS research', *Communications of the ACM*, vol. 31, no. 12, pp. 1502–505.

Jones, M. (1991) 'Post-industrial and post-fordist perspectives on information systems', *European Journal of Information Systems*, vol. 1, no. 2, pp. 171–82.

Keen, P. G. W. (1991) 'Relevance and rigour in information systems research: Improving quality, confidence, cohesion and impact', in Nissen, H-E, H. K. Klein, R. Hirschheim *Information Systems Research: Contemporary Approaches and Emergent Traditions* (Amsterdam: North Holland).

Klein, H. K. and M. D. Myers (1999) 'A set of principles for conducting and evaluating interpretive field studies in information systems', *MIS Quarterly*, vol. 23, no. 1, pp. 67–94.

Kuhn, T. (1960) *The Structure of Scientific Revolution* (Chicago: University of Chicago Press).

Lee, A. S. (1989) 'A scientific methodology for MIS case studies', *MIS Quarterly*, vol. 13, no. 1, pp. 33–50.

Lee, A. S. (1991) 'Integrating positivist and interpretive approaches to organizational research', *Organization Science*, vol. 2, no. 4, pp. 342–65.

Mason, R. O. and I. I. Mitroff (1973) 'A programme for research on management information systems', *Management Science*, vol. 19, no. 5 pp. 475–85.

Miles, M. B. and A. M. Huberman (1994) *Qualitative Data Analysis: An Expanded Sourcebook*. Thousand Oaks, CA: Sage.

Mingers, J. (2001) 'Combining IS research methods: Towards a pluralist methodology', *Information Systems Research*, vol. 12, no. 3, pp. 240–59.

Mumford, E., R. A. Hirschheim, G. Fitzgerald and A. T. Wood-Harper (eds) (1985) *Research Methods in Information Systems*. Proceedings of the IFIP WG 8.2 Colloquium, September 1984, Manchester. Amsterdam: North-Holland.

Ngwenyama, O. and A. Lee (1997) 'Communication richness in electronic mail: Critical social theory and the contextuality of meaning', *MIS Quarterly*, vol. 21, no. 2, pp. 145–67.

Nissen, H-E, H. K. Klein, and R. A. Hirschheim, (eds) (1991) *Information Systems Research: Contemporary Approaches and Emergent Traditions* (Amsterdam: North Holland).

Orlikowski, W. J. (1991) 'Integrated information environment or matrix of control? The contradictory implications of information technology', *Accounting Management and Information Technologies*, vol. 1, no. 1, pp. 9–42.

Orlikowski, W. J. and J. J. Baroudi (1991) 'Studying information technology in organizations: Research approaches and assumptions', *Information Systems Research*, vol. 2, no. 1, pp. 1–28.

Orlikowski, W. J. and D. Robey (1991) 'Information technology and the structuring of organizations', *Information Systems Research*, vol. 2, no. 2, pp. 143–71.

Popper, K. (1959) *The Logic of Scientific Enquiry* (London: Harper).

Remenyi, D. and B. Williams (1996) 'The nature of research: Qualitative or quantitative, narrative or paradigmatic?' *Information Systems Journal*, vol. 6, pp. 131–46.

Rosen, M. (1991) 'Coming to terms with the field: Understanding and doing organizational ethnography', *Journal of Management Studies*, vol. 28, no. 1, pp. 1–24.

Suchman, L. (1987) *Plans and Situated Actions: The Problem of Human-Machine Communication* (Cambridge: Cambridge University Press).

Vogel, D. R. and J. C. Wetherbe (1984) 'MIS research: A profile of leading journals and universities', *Data Base*, vol. 16, no. 3, pp. 3–14.

Walsham, G. (1993) *Interpreting Information Systems in Organizations* (Chichester: Wiley).

Walsham, G. (1995) 'The emergence of interpretivism in IS research', *Information Systems Research*, vol. 6, no. 4, pp. 376–94.

Zuboff, S. (1988) *In the Age of the Smart Machine* (New York: Basic Books).

5 The project and project management

- The project plan
- Formulating a realistic schedule
- Group projects
- Projects that go astray
- Example projects

If you can't plan it, you can't do it

Research projects have many characteristics in common with information systems development projects. However, it is surprising the number of students who are experts in the theory of information systems project management, but seem unable to 'practise what they preach' when it comes to managing their own research.

By definition, a research project is a 'once-off' affair with a definite start date and definite end date and, thus, like any other project (e.g. constructing a building) it needs a rather different form of management, compared to regular everyday tasks. If you are to deliver a satisfactory 'product' by the deadline, timing and organization are extremely important. You have various resources available to you, in particular, your own time and skills and these need to be managed carefully.

Any project comprises a number of different activities; some of these have to precede others while some can be performed in parallel. It is essential to meet the project deadline and the only way to be confident of achieving this is to plan out the project in advance. Many student projects have almost been ruined because the student spent too much time on the initial activities and had to rush the later parts; the reason, the lack of a project plan.

The project plan

Producing a project plan encourages completeness; it is an opportunity to 'think' your project through and seriously consider how long particular activities are going to take. With a plan, students can trace their progress as the weeks go by and recognize as soon as they start running late. With a project plan, it is also much less likely that an important task will be forgotten.

The plan should comprise a list of activities with planned execution dates. Each activity should produce a 'deliverable' (in terms of, for example, a recorded interview or a draft chapter). The first activity, then, is to identify the activities and their associated deliverables. These then need to be scheduled.

Needless to say, the plan itself should be formulated early on in the life of the project; it should not be produced as an afterthought towards the end. However, the plan needs to be related to the specific project in hand and thus cannot be drawn up properly before the project proposal has been accepted.

Just as with information systems development projects, the plan should comprise a number of stages. Some candidate stages are suggested by the previous chapter and the overall structure of this book. Thus, we would normally expect to see stages concerning project design or preparation (e.g., reading the background literature), data collection, data analysis and writing up. However, these may not be applicable for every project and the relative weighting between the stages will vary considerably between projects. Nevertheless, the notion of stages, with their completion seen as major project milestones, is a useful management concept for the completion of successful projects.

The milestones (ends of stage) of the plan will need to be tied to particular dates, with the key date being the submission deadline for the project. They may also match particularly important dates, such as Christmas, your birthday or the end of a college term. The actual estimation of the time needed for each stage will be difficult but should be approached realistically, as discussed in the following section.

Formulating a realistic schedule

It is clearly impossible to provide a single draft timetable that would suit every type of project. Box 5.1 below suggests some of the key issues that need to be addressed.

BOX 5.1

Key issues in developing a project plan

- Do not make the plan too detailed (KISS)
- Break the project down into achievable chunks of work
- Develop a schedule that ensures early concrete results
- Allow time at the end for writing up and revisions
- Try to build in some slack time – you will need it

Not having a plan is asking for trouble, but neither should a plan be too detailed; it should be no more than one A4 page. There is an old apposite saying: 'Keep it Simple, Stupid' (KISS). This means that you should not make your project (or your life) too complicated. A project is a piece of work that many people do, around the world, and managing a project is not 'rocket science'. The simple plan shown in Figure 5.1 below is at about the required level of detail. Note that this plan was prepared using a simple spreadsheet, not dedicated project management software such as Microsoft Project. While such systems may be of great use if you have really complex projects to manage, the danger in using them for a student-sized project is that all the bells and whistles that such packages allow will distract you from the basic structure of your work – usually just up to ten activities spread out over six to eight months. Having produced the plan, do not lose sight of it – pin it on the wall of your study or workroom and tick off the activities completed and the weeks passed as they are finished.

When developing the plan try to break the work down into manageable chunks that are achievable within two or three weeks. In this way you are in a better position to monitor your work. You will also be able to develop a good sense of progress, which should help your motivation. For this reason it makes good sense to structure a project in such a way that you are achieving solid results as soon as possible. This not only ensures that last minute problems (e.g., illness) do not put the success of the whole project in doubt, it also helps your motivation and sense of security. Certainly it is unwise to develop a project plan in such a way that everything depends on the last few activities. For example, in a software development project, use a top-down implementation strategy so that you can design and implement the user interface component independently from the database component. In a more analytical project, structure the work in such a way as to produce materials in early phases for direct incorporation in the final report.

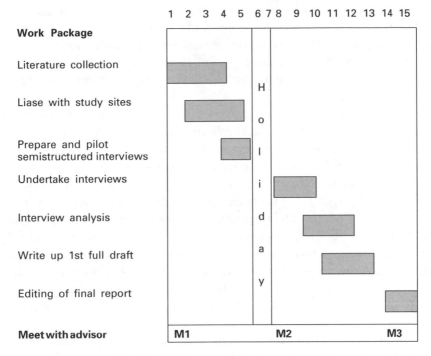

Figure 5.1   A project plan in diagrammatic form, shown 15 weeks of work.

The project plan has to take account of the dependencies between activities. For example; before an interview can be transcribed, it clearly has to be carried out and before it can be carried out, it has to be arranged. Some activities can proceed in parallel-for example, writing up the literature review and arranging interviews. The formulation of the plan has to take into account both the nature and dependencies of activities and is a non-trivial task itself.

Another important aspect of preparing a plan is allowing enough time at the end of the project for your adviser or mentor to read a full draft of the report and for you to take into account their comments. This means that the project work itself may well need to be completed up to one month before the deadline for submission, so as to allow time for drafting and revisions of the report. Also allow enough time at the end for final production of the report. It is surprising how long it takes to proof-read the final copy, to draw diagrams and tables, and to produce an attractive report layout. Even printing, photocopying and binding all take time, particularly where heavily used facilities are being shared within a college.

Finally, try to build in some slack. Some things will go wrong or take longer than originally expected. Thus, the plan should not be too rigid and should not be followed blindly. At the end of each stage, allow a couple of days for trivial tidying up. File away the papers you don't need, return the library books before they're overdue and clear your head a little. Mistakes tend to happen and things get missed out when you are working in a muddle. However, if you do diverge from the plan, especially if you start to run late, then reformulate the remainder of the plan to see what changes, if any, you have to make to the plan to finish on time.

The key point to emphasize, however, is the need for the schedule to be realistic, particularly regarding data collection (see Chapter 7), which involves much preparation and the involvement of many people and other factors outside the control of the student. For example, most students underestimate the time needed to prepare an effective postal questionnaire, which typically needs to go through a number of design iterations as questions are reworded and the layout refined. The preparation of a mailing list, printing the questionnaire, and 'stuffing' envelopes tend to take much longer than originally envisaged. In scheduling interviews, as well as taking account of the availability of interviewees, students should recognize that it is not normally effective (or feasible) to carry out more than two interviews in a day. Apart from the logistical problems of travelling between firms, interviews require the student to maintain a clear head.

It is all too easy when writing up interviews (or even carrying them out) for them to merge together and for the responses of the interviewees to become intermingled in the mind of the student.

Similarly, students should allow sufficient time for data analysis, which often requires considerable preparation before the analysis itself can be carried out. This may involve obtaining access to and/or learning how to use a statistical software package and entering large amounts of data. Days or weeks can easily slip by before any meaningful results are obtained.

You should start work on developing your ideas for a project as early as possible, sometimes even before the course proper starts. Although you may not wish to start work in earnest until the official start date, you can certainly begin thinking through the plan and brainstorming around some of the likely problem areas. It is very useful to begin preliminary tasks earlier. This is especially important if you need to write letters and wait for responses, or when you need to make special arrangements with a company or other organization. An early start is rarely a mistake.

Some types of project normally require an earlier starting date than others; for example, postal questionnaires usually require more lead-time than interviews. However, even an early start on interviews can be advantageous. If the student is approaching firms for the first time, they may require a written proposal and sufficient time to consider it before agreeing to participate. A more extreme case can be seen in a recent project, which sought to investigate information systems failures through a series of interviews. This is a very difficult topic on which to obtain reliable data as firms are not normally eager to reveal failures; it can be considered akin to 'washing one's dirty linen in public'. The student managed to get around this problem by reconceptualizing it as a search for factors that are important for success. With this stated objective, he made contact with firms very early on in the 'normal' project cycle and through repeated visits, was able to build up a sufficiently good relationship to tease out some of the 'skeletons in the cupboard'. The student also had to take care not to reveal any confidential data to the other firms, which meant producing various versions of the final report, depending upon their destination. This, in turn, required additional time spent on writing up. The project itself was very successful and all the parties concerned felt that they had gained from the exercise.

It is essential to discuss the plan with your adviser; in a 'walk-through', an experienced supervisor should be able to identify any feasibility problems. These may include too much or too little time allocated to an activity, a missing activity or the final draft appearing when the adviser is not available.

A few final suggestions: first, it is often a good idea to keep a special project diary or notebook. This is useful for noting relevant names and telephone numbers, new ideas, hints on hardware or software, and miscellaneous jottings. It is extremely easy to forget some of this key information and so, as soon as you have a new thought or receive some relevant information, note it down in the diary. When you have a slack period, browse through the diary to make sure that you have acted on all the appropriate notes.

Second, try to develop a steady rhythm and flow to your work. If possible, maintain regular hours for working on the project. The detail will depend a lot on individual circumstances but setting aside a number of regular blocks of two or three hours during the week usually provides a good time structure. Similarly, you will probably be dealing with hundreds of bits of paper (articles from the literature, interview transcripts, earlier versions of chapters, odd jottings) and these need to be controlled or else they will disappear or pop up in the wrong place. Thus, you need to develop a flow of paper around your workplace: this heap is to be worked on immediately, another heap has been processed but may be needed in the future, a third heap you don't know quite where it fits in, and so on. If some paper is rubbish, then throw it away. The same logic applies to computer files of your work in progress; they also need careful management.

Third, you must maintain regular back-ups of your work. Computer processors, cables and storage media have a habit of breaking down at crucial times and thieves do find laptops rather enticing. Thus you should develop a procedure for regular back-ups of your work to floppy disks or USB keys that you keep in a secure place and even hard copy back-ups can be used as a last resort.

Following the schedule

Having spent time and effort drawing up a project schedule, it makes no sense to file it away in a drawer and forget all about it. On the other hand, following it slavishly can result in a lifeless, 'mechanical' project. It is normally good practice to try to meet the major project milestones and allow more flexibility at a lower level. For example, just because the plan calls for five interviews does not mean that, in the event of a sixth interview arising, it should be rejected. That interview could be the key one that clinches the success of the project. Also, it may happen that the results of one of the other interviews may have to be discarded; perhaps because the cassette recorder was not working at the time or the interviewee misunderstood the questions or suddenly withdrew permission for the interview to be used. On the other hand, students should not find themselves in the position of being a month late in starting the data analysis.

Projects can threaten to run late because of host of internal and external factors. Background reading may be straightforward but it takes time. There may be difficulties locating the books or journals required and reading itself can be very time consuming. Students should also take care to recognize when to stop reading; it is surprisingly easy (and pleasant) to read around the same topic for months on end. On the other hand, further reading can often proceed in parallel with data collection and writing activities. Interviewees, supervisors and also the student concerned, may take a holiday, become ill or have to divert their attention to other activities (e.g., final year students may need to prepare for and attend lengthy job interviews). Libraries may close for stocktaking and college computer laboratories may shut down for redecoration or re-equipment.

In the event of a project starting to run late, there are two fatal strategies that students should avoid. These are the two extremes of unmitigated panic and chugging along as if nothing has happened. Panic is likely to result in unwise and arbitrary cuts in project activities solely to get it back on schedule. Such cuts are likely to damage the project by choking off the data collection, analysis or writing up of the project's raw material and thus reducing the quality of its content. On the other hand, pressing on regardless is likely to result in failure to meet the deadline. Students should calmly reconsider the activities remaining. Perhaps they can be rearranged to take advantage of slack time or possible parallelism (carrying out more than one activity at the same time). Some activities may need to be cut back but this decision should be made with care.

Importance of writing

It is essential to write draft sections as the project progresses. Do not leave the writing until the last weeks; it is too late by then. 'Writer's block', where the student becomes increasingly intimidated by blank sheets of paper, or transfixed by a blank screen, is a real danger, especially where the project is seen as a 'make or break' component of a degree course. This can be avoided if writing is started early, even if some of the initial text produced needs to be reworked later. Writing up your work as you progress will reveal gaps in understanding and provide opportunities for creativity. You must also appreciate that an adviser can only give final advice if he or she has seen a piece of work develop, so it is normally beneficial to show your adviser project chapters as they are written. Some advisers may prefer just to read in detail only a final draft but the opportunity to skim through chapters early on can help them to see exactly which direction a project is taking. For example, as advisers, we have seen projects that should have been theoretical reviews of a serious issue begin to turn into trivial software reviews, more suited to newsstand magazines than an academic dissertation. Early warnings of such problems allow students to be steered back on course.

Institutions, and perhaps even individual supervisors, will vary regarding the strictness of deadlines and the availability of extensions. It is normally wise to err on the side of safety and assume that extensions are not available, except perhaps in the case of illness. Academics are generally under increasing pressure to carry out their own research, as well as coping with increasing administrative tasks, such that extensions are becoming increasingly infeasible in an institution's crowded schedule. A common practice is to deduct marks for every day that a project submission is delayed, even where there is some justification for the delay. Rather than risking the project's success in such negotiations, just deliver it on time.

Group projects

It is quite common for students to be asked to work as a group on a collaborative project. The educational argument for including such project work within information systems courses is very strong. In working life almost all substantial activities are undertaken as team efforts, and there will seldom be an opportunity to work alone. This is particularly true of systems development activities, and thus it makes good sense for students to gain some experience of the problems and pitfalls of team based projects, and some of the approaches and techniques that are required to make them a success.

When group projects work well, they can deliver excellent work in which the whole is more than the sum of the parts. A good project group can exploit the particular talents of each member and use the debate and discussion within the group to refine and improve the quality of the work. Group work, when it goes well, will also provide an excellent experience and can build and cement friendships. However, when group projects breakdown, they can degenerate into profound ill-will and ugly clashes of ego – this happens in the 'real world' just as it does with student projects. There may be some groups that are just never going to work but, in our experience, most groups can be persuaded to work if certain clear guidance is given.

To succeed with a group project it is necessary to understand some of the key aspects of this type of work and the particular problems it poses. The first issue to grasp is that not all members of the group can participate in every task, and thus some decisions on work breakdown and responsibility are needed. Each member of the group will need to submit, to some degree, to the collective decisions of the group. To achieve this, and to monitor the work, the group's decisions will need to be made in a more explicit manner than is perhaps necessary for a lone researcher. Once decisions are made, each member of the group then has to honour the implied contract in delivering their contribution within the overall structure of the work, and within the agreed timescale.

It will often be the case that students are given a free choice in deciding who they will work with on a group project. If this is the case then we suggest that you pause before signing up to work with your closest friends. First of all, they may not be your friends at the end of the experience; more seriously, the choice of people to work with needs to be made with care. You need to understand your own strengths and weaknesses and appreciate what other people can bring to a project. For example, a project team may need people with diverse characteristics: a native English speaker for preparing written materials, a computer enthusiast for software development, a 'people person' to deal with users, a library burrower to locate elusive material, and so on. The really canny student can see these needs and identify who has the potential to satisfy them, and then builds a project team on this basis.

Team structures

The need for explicit decision making means that group projects need to be organized around formal meetings. Such meetings will need to have a clear agenda – a sequence of items to be discussed - and after the meeting a set of minutes may need to be written up and circulated. These minutes can provide a record of what was discussed and decided at the meeting. Productive meetings are best held in somewhat formal surroundings. If possible book a classroom or meeting room, rather than trying to meet in the library, cafeteria or bar. A meeting room should also have facilities such as a white-board or flip-chart, which can help to ensure a focused group discussion.

Such formal meetings will need to be held from time to time, in the early stages to establish the project, later on to monitor and adjust work activities, and at the end to refine the final output. Between meetings it may be useful for a project group to meet more informally and briefly to exchange information on progress. Some such information exchange can also be achieved by using such facilities as electronic mail or a shared database of documents.

Planning and explicit structure for the work is then the key, but this needs to be supported by explicit structure for the team itself. This structure might be achieved in various ways. Two broad possibilities usually present themselves. The first approach is to allocate substantive areas of work to individual members of the team – structure by topic. The second is to allocate specific roles to team members – structure by task. When the work involves considerable uncertainty or the members are particularly unskilled at the task, it may be more effective to allocate areas or tasks to pairs of team members.

In a project organized by topic, the allocation of responsibilities is driven by the subject matter. If the topic is, for example, computer supported cooperative work (CSCW), then an allocation might be in terms of CSCW software products, development methods, benefits and evaluation issues, and CSCW case studies. With a division along these lines, and some broad guidance on the deliverable required – say 1500 words each, each group member can work more or less independently in the early phases of the work. There will then come a time when the individual contributions need to be combined, but if the breakdown of topics has been well structured, and the individual briefs have been followed, then this should be a fairly straightforward process.

Organizing projects by task implies giving each group member a specific responsibility within the overall process. Thus, within a group, there may be roles for a project manager who coordinates the work, a scribe or editor who is responsible for the written output, a researcher who collects data, an analyst to process data and perhaps a presenter to make an oral presentation. The nature of the project topic will suggest particular roles, and within a larger project it may be possible to rotate the roles as phases are completed. This task or role based means of organizing a project group can be very efficient, but it does require that the members of the group respect the roles that others occupy. In our experience particular problems can arise if the person taking on the project manager role sees this as a position of power and an opportunity to criticize the work of others. That is not the role of a project manager in real organizations and it should not be the role in a student project.

Projects that go astray

Projects go wrong in many ways: the original objective turns out to be too difficult; access to some vital information is denied; or perhaps the software does not work. When part of a project goes wrong, it is of course worrying, but that does not necessarily mean that the course (or degree) is immediately failed. A project should be designed in such a way that it is robust and does not depend on the success of any one part. Students have to expect some setbacks along the way and be prepared to make appropriate responses.

Sometimes a project that goes wrong can be seen as an opportunity. Why did it go wrong? What does that tell you? Is there a good story to be told? In our experience students can often find a new beginning for a project within the wreckage of the old. This typically requires a 'cool head' on the part of the student and perhaps the advice of a more experienced researcher. The following examples of projects that 'went wrong' are based on our personal experience and demonstrate how, with a little extra thought, success can be snatched from the jaws of disaster.

Problems with politics

The first example concerns a project undertaken by a student for a large public body. The initial project was to develop a design for a database system that would be used by the personnel office to prepare job advertisements and to deal with the resulting job applications. The student was half-way through the project when he discovered that there already existed another design for the system, prepared by a rival department, and furthermore there was a standard commercial software package tailor-made for the job. At first he felt disheartened to have been involved in what was a political ploy by a department that was using him to show that they too could 'come up with the technical stuff'. On further reflection however the student was able to redirect his project to consider the management structures used by this organization to direct its information technology activities, and to suggest how they might be improved. The project report was good and told the whole story; the really happy ending came when they offered him a job on the basis of his insightful analysis of what they were doing wrong.

Another student managed to gain entry to an international investment bank, with permission to study the trends towards decentralization of information systems and their management. She had only just started her interviews when a senior manager gave a rather unwise interview to the media, which upset one of the bank's major customers. The manager was quickly sacked but this incident caused most of the other managers to withdraw from the planned interviews with the student. She was thus only able to study one of the many divisions of the bank. However, studying this division revealed not only the predicted trend away from traditional centralized systems and centralized management towards more decentralized approaches, it also showed a more recent move towards recentralization, which had not been anticipated. This evidence, although based on only a single division, allowed the student to return to the mainstream literature and reconceptualize it, based on this notion of recentralization. Thus, her project, which turned out to be highly successful, was much more conceptual and less empirical than the original proposal.

Somebody has been here before

In a recent project on outsourcing, the student found that other researchers who had just published an excellent report of their study had covered his topic. The student's focus was originally on the management and control of outsourced information systems and services and it seemed initially that 'the rug had been pulled out' from under him. However, by concentrating upon in-depth case studies, the student was able to use the published work as an up-to-date foundation for his work. From this he was able to add increased depth and breadth, producing not only a fine piece of empirical work but also a valuable critique of the published study.

There's nothing here

A recent student project concerned the implementation of an ERP (enterprise resource planning) system into a Greek bank's human resource department. The student (and supervisor) expected to find a conflict between the standardized technocratic software and the 'touchy feely' staff of HR. However, when he arrived the student found that the implementation had barely begun and only a handful of staff were using a few non-controversial functions of the system. The expected 'story' just wasn't there.

After some thought and discussion with his supervisor, the student changed tack and investigated why the ERP implementation had been delayed. He found that there were problems with implementing the system across the bank and produced a good project that analysed these problems.

Data collection disasters

A few years ago, a student intending to carry out a survey based on postal questionnaires in Ireland was faced with a long-running postal strike. There seemed to be no prospect of the strike ending quickly and meanwhile time was slipping by. This student solved this problem by sending out the questionnaires by fax, which involved additional work in obtaining respondents' fax numbers as well as many hours crouched over the fax machine feeding in the questionnaires. This was before 'junk faxes' became a menace and, impressed by his ingenuity, a relatively high proportion of respondents replied (also by fax).

Another example of a student coping with data collection problems concerns a survey carried out by postal questionnaire in Greece. For various reasons, the questionnaire was sent out very late, so that the companies received it during early August. Unfortunately, this is the time when industry and commerce in Greece virtually grinds to a halt as most people leave for holidays. In August, Greek companies operate with a skeleton staff who have neither the time nor the inclination to complete questionnaires. Luckily, the student herself was in Greece at the time (on holiday!) and was able to use her father's connections to increase the otherwise abysmal response rate. These family connections also allowed her to gain access to relevant organizations very quickly and to supplement the postal questionnaire with some useful case studies.

Technical problems

An obvious danger that should be guarded against is the loss or corruption of large parts of the electronic version of the report or data. Students should be wary of disk failures and viruses and always keep a back-up copy in a safe place. Institutions do tend to replace machines and 'spring clean' hard disks especially during the summer. It is very easy to leave a floppy disk inside a laboratory machine and only notice its loss a few days later. Even hard-copy is not necessarily safe; students have left their one and only copy of a project on trains, aeroplanes, in bars, and in the flats of discarded boyfriends. Projects have even been 'lost' by institutions themselves.

Going the distance

Unfortunately, while some projects can be turned around and 'put back on the rails', others manage to snatch disaster from the jaws of success. Recently a student was doing a project in the area of corporate social responsibility and he was very worried about how he could obtain interviews with senior information systems managers with knowledge in the field. He had a lucky break and early on in the project he interviewed one such manager who was very helpful and gave him various contacts, as well as a mass of useful views, information and opinions. However, perhaps from a sense of false security with the ease of the first interview, instead of following this trail immediately the student allowed himself to be distracted by other things. When he returned to the project, after a few weeks, he found that the contacts had gone on holiday and both he and the project had lost momentum.

Other versions of this problem involve 'starting too late' and 'losing interest'. Psychologically, starting a project is a big step and it is too easy to keep putting it off until 'tomorrow'. With a fixed deadline and a substantial effort required to carry out the work, it is normally extremely difficult to recover from a late start. Students may be lucky in finding information quickly and can cut back on their leisure time and sleeping hours but the final product usually reflects this in its sloppiness and lack of depth. As such, it represents a waste of talent and effort.

Losing interest is a common problem, especially with projects that extend for more than a few months. After a while, students find their initial enthusiasm to be waning. They may begin to think that their project is boring and that maybe they should have chosen a different topic or they may encounter difficulties with the people or material that they are dealing with. This may be the time to talk about it to their supervisor, or to a friend. Most students go through a difficult patch during projects but usually things work out. There is a job to be done and they just have to knuckle down and do it, through thick and thin. It is times like this when the benefit of building in slack time in the project plan really shows through. Taking a weekend off and 'recharging the batteries' can be very helpful but is difficult if the time is just not available.

Sometimes, contrary to the project plan, projects build up their own momentum (or lack of) and take on their own direction. It is not always obvious when a project is 'going wrong'. It may be difficult for a student to decide whether they are following up valuable leads and 'going with the flow' or whether the project is veering off course and heading for oblivion. This is where the input of an experienced advisor can prove to be invaluable.

Finally, although research projects are academic pieces of work, which require a high level of intellectual input, understanding and creativity, they equally require to be managed. One of the main causes of projects going astray is simply a failure to keep an eye on the evolving situation. If they are to be completed effectively and on time, due consideration must be given to planning, scheduling and monitoring progress. In our experience, projects are more likely to fail from a lack of project management than any intellectual inadequacies on the part of the student or through catastrophic 'acts of God'. A (true) old saying is that 'projects become late one day at a time'. Left alone, projects tend to wander like lost souls in the wilderness. They need to be managed actively.

Example projects

The last section of this chapter is devoted to a selection of example projects from our direct experience. These examples are based on projects which we have seen students undertake in the recent past. They are not intended to be taken as a list of recommended topics or approaches, but to indicate a range of possibilities and a variety of approaches that might be taken. The examples also offer some insights into what can go right and what can go wrong in project work. Each case is based on one or more real projects, but we have taken the liberty to change some details here and there to make particular points or to protect the innocent.

Project: e-business in the automotive sector

This project was carried out, as an MSc project, a few years ago when e-business was very fashionable and the dot.com companies were on the crest of their wave. The student managed to get into a new division of a large automotive manufacturer, which had been set up specifically to develop e-business. The staff were mostly young and enthusiastic and were eager to describe to her their strategy and plans for the future. Combining their views with the literature, and adding a sound critical analysis, gave her a distinction grade for her MSc project. Starting with these contacts, she returned to the company to extend the study as the main part of her PhD research. By this time, the new division was running into various difficulties as the e-business climate deteriorated and eventually the division closed down. Through good fortune, she found herself there at the birth, through the operation and at the death of the new division. This made an excellent 'story' for her PhD and supports the saying: *'Big oaks grow from little acorns'*. We know of many other MSc projects that have led, intentionally or unintentionally, to successful PhDs in areas as diverse as electronic data interchange (EDI) and information systems and Islamic banking.

Project: A review of the national IT policy of a particular country

In this project the student sought to document and comment on the policy directions that her country had taken with regard to information technology over the previous ten years. This included consideration of the overall development targets of the country and their place within them of information technology. Among the policy areas that she addressed were: education policy, the labour market and skill requirements; laws and regulations; incentives for multinational companies; telecommunications infrastructure (national and international); the local hardware and software sectors.

This was a good topic. There was much material available in newspapers, magazines, and in government publications. She also went to the academic literature and reviewed a number of scholarly studies of the role of IT in development in general, and in her own country and region, and supplemented this with interviews with politicians and administrators.

However, unfortunately, the final report was not as good as it could have been because she was unable to bring much original critical analysis to bear. Most of the themes in the project report were based on a single-minded and optimistic view of the benefits of IT to the country. Few of the problems or more complex issues were addressed, despite the fact that she had found a good deal of such material during her research.

Project: Website evaluation

Rather than a single project, this topic led to a small 'cluster' of projects. Some research was going on in the department concerning the general problem of evaluating websites. However, such evaluations need to be context sensitive; that is, the industry and the country concerned need to be taken into account. For example, it may not be particularly meaningful to compare in detail a bank's website with that of a local social services department. Hence, this gave rise to various student projects that evaluated websites in different contexts; for example, Greek banks, Thai retailers, UK local government and (worldwide) airlines.

Despite their common source, some of these projects were much more successful than others. It was necessary to adapt the evaluation instrument to the context as well as to provide a discussion as to how the technology and the context had interacted together to result in the websites concerned. Some students were much more able at these tasks than other students. The students generally enjoyed being part of this informal research team, each with their own context to contend with. They probably all gained from the exchange of literature and experience but there was sufficient 'clear water' between the individual projects to make them stand on their own.

Another area where such a 'cluster' strategy worked well was in considering the 'digital divide' between the information rich and the information poor. Individual students could apply similar concepts to very different contexts; for example, inner city ghettoes, rural parts of developing countries and divides based on gender or age. Nevertheless, care always needs to be taken that the final projects are the work of individual students and any 'free-riders' are spotted early on.

Project: An IT strategy study for a shipping company

In this project a student started by studying and documenting the existing information systems in a firm of ship managers. This was not a simple task because the company had allowed their systems to grow on a piecemeal basis, and nobody really knew what systems were in place or in use (some were in place but never used!). The conclusion that he came to was that this company was muddling along from day to day without a medium or long term IT plan. The second part of the project was then to make a start on such a plan.

The target audience for the student's work was the general manager, who was a very sensible and successful businessman, but who knew nothing about IT. The report he produced therefore had to explain in quite simple language the role of information systems and the challenge of managing them. The report had to make its points in terms of a business case for a different approach to IT within this company. The student found supporting material in the literature on information systems management and information systems strategy. He also studied the specialist shipping literature to find out about new developments in the business environment within which the company worked.

The final result was a project that was clearly valuable to the client – for the first time there was an overall catalogue of the existing systems within the company. Furthermore each system was described and evaluated in terms of its technical quality, business utility and actual usage.

Project: An analysis of the requirements for an information system to support the maintenance manager of a food retailing chain

This project used Peter Checkland's (1981, 1990) soft systems methodology (SSM) as the basis for a study of a particular business problem within a large supermarket chain. The student had worked in the company during vacations, and was able to persuade her previous boss to allow her to do a study of a particularly messy problem involving many people. You can read one account of some of the work in Avgerou and Cornford (1998).

In order to undertake the project she had to interview various people a number of times. She had to keep good records of these conversations, and to report on her work to the project sponsor from time to time. In adopting SSM as her approach she also had to study the literature on this method, and make a case for its use. At the end of the work she was able to assess SSM, and describe those areas in which she judged that it had worked well and those areas where she judged that it had not worked. The final report was thus in two main parts: the case study for the maintenance system itself, and a commentary and critique on SSM.

Project: Repetitive strain injury

Being in 'the right place at the right time' and seizing every opportunity can be very helpful when students are carrying out research projects. Around ten years ago, one of our students chose to study repetitive strain injury (RSI) for her research project. This was a very timely choice of a topic because compensation cases were just coming to court and the European Union directive concerning health and safety had just been published. This meant that both employers and trade unions were keen to gain information in this area. As part of the project the student prepared a questionnaire, and the level of interest in the topic ensured that she received a good response. She also obtained a number of useful interviews with managers responsible for formulating policy in this area and trade union officials who represented RSI sufferers.

While carrying out the project, she watched a television programme concerning RSI. She carefully noted the name and location of a local medical specialist who appeared on the programme, and telephoned him a few days later to ask for an interview. Although he did not wish to give such an interview, he invited her to sit-in at one of his clinics to observe the process of diagnosis and treatment. This was an opportunity that the student had created and expertly seized. The resulting project report was marked very highly, and a version was later published as a paper in an academic journal (Khilji and Smithson, 1994).

Project: Hotel information systems

While the student in the case above revelled in the context of her project, taking to it like a 'duck to water', and making many useful friends and contacts in the course of her work, this does not always happen. A much less happy example comes from many years ago when a student chose to study the information systems in a medium-sized London hotel. As well as investigating the technical systems, she was keen to analyse the working climate in terms of job satisfaction and industrial democracy. At the time, many of the staff in such hotels were working illegally and partly because of this their pay and working conditions were very poor.

The student was genuinely appalled at what she regarded as Dickensian practices and castigated the hotel management bitterly in her report. When he read the report, the hotel manager angrily telephoned the head of the department, threatening legal action. Fortunately, he calmed down when it was pointed out to him that the hotel was likely to be damaged by any adverse publicity that such a case would draw. Disregarding any doubts about the legality and morality of the hotel's employment regime – and these practices were common in many hotels – the student had not fitted well into the research context. The project report itself was not very good, and the critique of the working conditions took no account of the overall social context and showed a limited capacity for analytical thinking.

Project: Telecommunication services

This project was concerned with the developing market for certain types of information services delivered through value added networks. This was an industry with a small number of key players working within a tight regulatory regime. The project was aimed at exploring the emerging structure of this industry and the strategy of the various players. To do this the student arranged a number of interviews with managers in the main companies. They were in general happy to see her, and were able to provide a great deal of useful information and direct her to documentary sources.

One manager in particular was very helpful. He devoted a good deal of time to the student, and offered a lot of constructive advice. However, as time went on, the student began to be concerned. She realised that this manager was carefully constructing questions for her to ask of people from his main competitors. In this way he hoped to discover critical aspects of their strategy in this emerging market. Once the student realised what was happening she discussed the situation with her project adviser. Following the adviser's recommendation she politely withdrew from close cooperation with the particular manager, and completed the project on her own.

The resulting project report did not explicitly refer to this situation, but it did make some interesting comments on the nature of the competitive and regulatory regime, which was based to some degree on reflections on this experience.

Summary

- Projects need to be planned, but not everything will go according to the plan, and some revisions will be needed.
- Plans provide a work breakdown structure and a control mechanism to enable you to monitor your progress.

- Write draft sections as the project progresses – don't leave all the writing to the end.
- Group projects require particularly careful planning and need explicit project team structures.
- Sometimes, despite the most careful planning, things go seriously awry. If they do, step back and reassess the situation. It may be that there is an opportunity waiting to be seized.

Further reading

Over the years, a number of useful books have appeared concerned with helping students to manage their research projects. These include the following, all of which we believe have something to offer. However, we would caution against reading too much about the research process. We feel that most students, especially those with good supervisors, do need to get out and engage with the research itself. For many, the countdown to the project deadline has already begun and action is needed!

Bell, J. (1999) *Doing Your Research Project: A Guide for First-Time Researchers in Education and Social Science* (Milton Keynes: Open University Press).

Blaxter, L., C. Hughes, and M. Tight (2001) *How to Research* (Milton Keynes: Open University Press).

Howard, K. and J. A. Sharp (2002) *The Management of a Student Research Project* Aldershot: Gower.

Saunders, M., P. Lewis, and A. Thornhill (2002) *Research Methods for Business Students* FT Prentice Hall.

Wisker, G. (2001) *The Postgraduate Research Handbook* (London: Palgrave).

References

Avgerou, C. and T. Cornford (1998) *Developing Information Systems: Concepts, Issues and Practice* (London: Macmillan).

Checkland, P. (1981) *Systems Thinking, Systems Practice* (Chichester: Wiley).

Checkland, P. and J. Scholes (1990) *Soft Systems Methodology in Action* (Chichester: Wiley).

Khilji, N and S. Smithson (1994) 'Repetitive strain injury in the UK: Soft tissues and hard issues', *International Journal of Information Management*, vol. 14, pp. 95–108.

6 Using research literature

- ■ **Using libraries and other information resources**
- ■ **Using and citing references**
- ■ **Plagiarism**
- ■ **The literature review**

All projects will need to contain some references to the existing literature. If a project is very practical or technical – for example largely analysis, design or programming – there is still a need to explore relevant literature and to reference sources that are used to get ideas or that provide the basis for a design methodology. If a project is more descriptive or analytical, if it relates to how things happen in the world and how people feel or think about them, it will certainly need to draw on many sources of information and ideas, and hence to include more references. Usually it is appropriate to include a literature review section early in a project report so as to provide a baseline of understanding of other work in the topic area and to identify how this particular study fits in.

Using libraries and other information resources

In the first edition of this book we could confidently write, 'The first place to start a search for literature on any given topic is in an appropriate library.' Today this position is not so easy to maintain if we just mean to enter into a library building; for many people the first place to go to locate information is to the Internet and to use a search engine such as Google (www.google.com). We have more to say about using the Internet below, but for the moment we want to emphasise that libraries and the library resources they provide are still of utmost importance and in the end are far easier to navigate and offer more to somebody undertaking a research project than the wild anarchic world of the Internet at large. Nevertheless, when you do 'go' to a library that probably does not mean walking along the shelves and scanning the titles of books – interesting as that may be. It may not even mean pushing open the doors and entering the specific building where books are held. The holdings of most academic libraries of any size are now catalogued using computers and the primary means of locating material will be through an interactive search that you can usually do from anywhere in the world with access to a networked computer. Still, do remember, if the topic is likely to have relevant material from before the early 1990s, it is worthwhile checking how far back the comprehensive computerization of the catalogue you are using has gone, since many libraries still retain the earlier, card-based system for older material.

Even if you are working in a physical library you may find in the early stages of a project that the 'scanning the shelves method' is particularly unhelpful in the area of information systems since the books that represent the subject are highly unlikely to be shelved or classified together. Although a student of say, statistics, can reasonably expect to find the bulk of materials co-located, the student of information systems certainly should not, and titles may be spread around under the broad headings of computers, information technology, management, sociology, industrial relations and so on. You will soon see why using a computerized catalogue is essential.

When using a computerized catalogue, there are a number of ways to proceed. Most catalogues allow searches by some mix of author, title or phrases in the title, cataloguing classification (Library of Congress or Dewey – the class marks used to organize books on the shelves), date of publication and keywords. Such catalogues are usually restricted to books, official reports and perhaps the main title of journals (but not the individual articles within a journal). On the other hand, you may be lucky and work in a library that has the most up-to-date systems which can provide search capabilities that span books, reports and journal articles.

The obvious starting point for a search may be to use keywords or phrases, for example 'group decision aid systems'. This may reveal a huge number of titles, or it may reveal none. If the number is huge, then some refinement of the search may be called for; perhaps titles published since 1998. If the result is no titles or very few titles, then perhaps the keywords used need to be refined. In order to do this it is a good idea to inspect the catalogue record of a few books that you do know are relevant and to see what keywords are used to describe them. This makes particular sense when you realize that often the keywording is done within a restricted controlled vocabulary, and your search term of 'group decision aid systems' may not be a part of this vocabulary whereas 'group decision support' may be.

As you search it is a good idea to note down the classification numbers for the materials located. Of course, this is needed to locate the books on the shelf, but more interestingly, it can help to provide an interdisciplinary map of the area of study – perhaps books classified as management, industrial relations, computer science, economics and psychology may turn up as a search on 'group decision support' progresses.

An online catalogue of current holdings is not the only resource that you might expect to find in a library. There will be many other online information resources, including comprehensive general digital library resources that cover both books and journal literature – for example *Ebsco Premier, Science Direct* or *ABI Global*, as well as commercial online resources from traditional publishers and specialist bibliographies for particular topics. You may also have access online to a citation index such as *ISI Web of Knowledge* which, given a particular author or article, allows you to find out *other* publications that have cited it. This can be a very powerful way of following up a topic as it is debated in the academic literature.

Such online resources can be particularly useful to track down all the published works of a known authority in a particular field and, depending on the subscriptions a particular library has, may allow you to directly download and print the material. For example *Ebsco Premier*, one of the market leaders, will allow you access to articles from many journals and magazines including *Harvard Business Review* and most of the leading information systems journals listed below. A useful article by Schwartz and Russo (2004) published in the *Communications of the ACM* gives a considered analysis of the availability of 50 top information systems journals in a number of commercially available databases. However, the world of online publishing is changing rapidly and new business models are being tried out all the time by established publishers and newcomers to the market (perhaps the opportunity for a project?), so any information given here may change over time. It is certainly a good idea, at the start of your project work, to devote some time to exploring just what is available from your institution's library, and learning how to make the best use if it.

Journals and Conferences

When looking for information for a project, you may initially be attracted to books. However, in many cases (and this will depend upon the nature of a project), books are either too elementary, too old or else give a much too general treatment of a topic. You will find that articles in academic journals are often preferable; they are typically much more focused and concise, as well as being up-to-date. Academic journals are the main medium for the dissemination of the results of academic research so if you want to be up-to-date that is where you need to look.

There are a growing number of journals devoted to information systems, and it is very hard to set down a definitive list. Schwartz and Russo (2004) give a ranked list of the top 50 (based on work by Mylonopoulos and Theoharakis (2001)), but this is a listing rather biased towards journals from the United States. Among the most relevant, well respected and widely cited journals with a broad coverage are the following (note their rankings by Mylonopoulos and Theoharakis when available are given in brackets):

- *Communications of the ACM (2)*
- *European Journal of Information Systems (11)*
- *Information and Management (10)*
- *Information Systems Journal (16)*
- *Information Systems Research (3)*
- *Information Technology and People (27)*
- *Journal of Information Technology (-)*
- *Journal of Strategic Information Systems (20)*
- *MIS Quarterly (1)*
- *The Information Society (36)*

The *Communications of the ACM* (CACM) is strictly speaking a magazine, but it does contain useful summary and survey articles that present brief accounts of contemporary research. The American Association for Computing Machinery (ACM www.acm.org), its publishers, also publish a large number of more specialized journals in the field of computer science and information systems, for example *ACM Transactions on Information Systems*, and *Data Base*, the journal of their special interest group on business data processing. Similarly the American Institute for Electrical and Electronic Engineers (IEEE) Computer Society (www.computer.org) publish a range of journals and magazines. Their magazine format publications, such as *IEEE Computer, IEEE Software, IEEE Micro* and *IEEE Expert* are often useful starting points for research, with short and accessible articles summarizing current developments in their respective fields. Both the ACM and the IEEE make all their publications available online at a very modest cost, either as an institutional subscription or to individual members. Student membership of these organisations may be well worthwhile just for this service, and also brings other benefits. The Association for Information Systems (www.aisnet.org) also has modest student membership rates and publish two online journals, the

Communications of the AIS and the *Journal of the AIS*. These two are only available online, with no paper versions produced.

ACM Computing Surveys is a publication of the ACM that contains just review articles that summarize and structure the existing state of the art in various fields of computing. Not all issues contain papers on mainstream information systems topics; some are very much concerned with computer science, but from time to time there are relevant papers. As just two examples, the December 2001 edition contains a 47 page paper by Ivory and Hearst entitled, 'The State of the Art in Automating Usability Evaluation of User Interfaces', a paper that has over 133 references to other material (Ivory and Hearst, 2001) and the March 2003 edition contains a 28 page article by Dedrick, Gurbaxani and Kraemer entitled 'Information Technology and Economic Performance: A Critical Review of the Empirical Evidence' which contains 84 references to other works (Dedrick, Gurbaxani and Kraemer, 2003). Many other journals also carry survey articles from time to time. For example, *MIS Quarterly* in 2001 contained a comprehensive survey of knowledge management by Alavi and Leidner (2001) and *Accounting, Management and Information Technology* published a useful review titled 'Information Technology and Organisational Learning' (Robey, Boudreau and Rose, 2000). It is very worth while to search for such review articles early on in your research because they can provide a rapid route into the subject and usually offer many signpost to other relevant works.

In addition, and reflecting the multi-disciplinary nature of information systems, management-oriented articles often appear in management journals such as the *Harvard Business Review* and the *Sloan Management Review*. It is also probably the case that your project topic should lead you to more specific and narrowly focused journals that will contain relevant material. For example, if your project is concerned with man–machine interface aspects, then the *International Journal of Human–Computer Studies, Behaviour and Information Technology*, or *Interacting with Computers* might be relevant. In the area of software engineering you may find *Software Practice and Experience* and the *Software Engineering Journal* helpful. Areas such as e-commerce and e-government have also given rise to their own journals, for example, *EM-Electronic Markets*, or *International Journal of E-Commerce*. You can be quite certain, what ever your project area, that there will be some specialised journal out there, and you need to take some time to try to track it down.

Academic debate does not only take place within published journals. It is also very much alive within the numerous conferences held around the world. Some are very large with over 1000 people attending, and almost all publish a conference proceeding containing the various papers that are presented. These proceedings are usually available electronically from one or other academic body, for example the IEEE, ACM or AIS. Among the most prominent and largest general conferences in the field of information systems are:

- International Conference on Information Systems (ICIS)
- European Conference on Information Systems (ECIS)
- Americas Conference on Information Systems (AMCIS)
- Pacific Conference on Information Systems (PACIS)
- Hawaii International Conference on Systems Science (HICSS)

It is a real advantage of working in the field of information systems and studies of technology that most of the literature you will seek out is quite recent, and most recent material, including all the journals and conferences cited above, are available online. Your library may have paper copies on the shelf, but they are more likely to have electronic access. This means that you can access material directly, and print it out without worrying about whether it is actually on the shelf or being used by another person. You will certainly need to work a bit to gain the information on what is available through your library, and how to gain access to it, perhaps needing special passwords but in the longer run acquiring and practicing such skills will serve you well.

The Internet and ISWorld Net

Apart from formal academic journals the Internet now provides a huge (some would say infinite) pool of information, propaganda, gossip and exhibitionism. Finding things there, however, is not easy, or at least it is not easy to know exactly what you have found. For example, typing 'ERP implementation' – a good potential topic for a project – into the ACM portal I get over 200 references, but I can be fairly sure that most of them are potentially useful. They come from the publications of a reputable scientific society, they have been peer reviewed for the most part by other experts and I am fairly confident that they are not (overtly) selling me anything. Each article will have a brief abstract that I can review and they will all be catalogued using key word. If I type the same phrase into Google I certainly get well over 200 links, but most of them are of dubious quality, and many (most) are trying to sell me something. When we did this exercise preparing this book we found on the first page just one possibly useful link, to *CIO Magazine* (www.cio.com), with a joke – just about good enough to pass it on here – but probably not the basis for a research project (See Box 6.1).

We then suggest that, for a researcher, Google and other general Internet search engines are useful tools, they do allow you to find a *particular* thing if you know it is out there, but they are of far less help in collecting together materials of known quality. At the start of your project you may feel that

---

ERP implementation in ten Easy Steps

1. Ask the board of directors for an arbitrary but large sum of money. (Suggestion: $300 million.)
2. Give half the money to consultants. Ask them to select an appropriate ERP package for your company. Consultants will audit your business processes for six months and then select SAP, which they happen to resell.
3. Form cross-functional implementation teams. Hold meetings.
4. Reengineer all your business processes to match the software's model.
5. Give the other half of the money to consultants.
6. Install the software.
7. Train end users repeatedly.
8. Cross your fingers.
9. Turn on the software.
10. If you're still in business, immediately return to Step one because its time for an upgrade.

Source: From CIO magazine, 1 April 2001.

Google is your best friend, but beware. You will certainly have to exercise a lot of critical judgement as you wade through the material you find, and you probably would be better off starting your research with more formal and structured resources.

For this reason we have emphasised other possible Internet and online resources that you may want to use, including library catalogues, digital library resources and online journals, the sites of major publishers of academic work, such as ACM or IEEE. There is another valuable site for IS researchers at ISWorld Net (www.isworld.org) ISWorld Net is an activity of the Association of Information Systems (AIS). It is a collaborative effort to support the creation and dissemination of knowledge on information systems and is managed and run by an international group of academics and practitioners. Their mission is stated as follows on their web site:

> We will provide information management scholars and practitioners with a single entry point to resources related to information systems technology and promote the development of an international information infrastructure that will dramatically improve the world's ability to use information systems for creating, disseminating, and applying knowledge.

Among the divisions within ISWorld Net are sections devoted to research and scholarship, teaching and learning, professional activities and country specific pages. These latter may be very useful for students studying overseas and who want to keep in touch with information systems within their own, perhaps very different, home context. The research and scholarship section is a good source of information on many methodological issues and contains various groups of resources to support researchers in different areas including detailed bibliographies and summary materials.

ISWorld Net also provides information about electronic versions of journals and many other publications in information systems. This is also a place to find a listing of Information Systems Departments and Research Centres around the world, many of which publish online research working papers – one good way to get hold of up-to-date research material.

Other sources

Other publications, including newspapers and business publications can also provide a useful source of research information. Publications such as *The Financial Times, The Economist, The Wall Street Journal, The Far East Economic Review* or *Business Week* all contain regular material on information systems issues, as do the myriad of computer industry magazines. It is important, however, to judge the quality and status of such publications, and make certain that you are not just quoting second-hand press releases or vendors' propaganda. With on-line services it is relatively easy to locate articles in the press, and often it is possible to 'down-load' the text directly. For example, if your project demands an analysis of the history of IBM in the past decade, your raw material, in the form of *Wall Street Journal* stories over the period, can be available in seconds. Your job is then to read through the half a million or so words that this may represent! So, the time saving in locating material may be offset by the time to filter and assimilate it.

Finally we should note that Internet sources of all kinds pose a problem in providing good citations. When using the Internet we need to understand that the information we find and use may be there today, but be gone (or revised) tomorrow. Nonetheless, it is good practice to give the URL for any information that is used, just as you would provide a full citation for a book or journal article. The convention is to provide the date of access as well as the date of publication. Thus the extract from *CIO Magazine* given above would have a full citation as follows:

Slater, D (2001) "ERP Implementation in 10 Easy Steps", *CIO Magazine*. April 1st. Available at http://www.cio.com/archive/040101/tl_erp.html. Last accessed 13 Jan 2005

Using and citing references

With the aid of a good library and on-line searching any researcher should be able to rapidly develop a substantial list of references to source material of one kind or another. A sensible researcher takes great care to manage this information; the critical issue is to capture the information once and once only. If this is not done, then days can be wasted in the final phases of a project in confirming or completing half-noted references. When you read a useful book or journal article, it is essential to make brief notes *at the time*. These should include the ideas that you intend to use, plus the bibliographic (catalogue) details that you will need to include in the references section at the end of the project. A handy way of keeping this information is through the use of some form of note cards, with the bibliographic details on one side and the content aspects on the other. Even if you use a bibliographic software package to maintain this data, you will probably need to keep some written notes. Indeed the computer has as yet provided no really satisfactory substitute for note cards for use in structuring ideas and organizing streams of thought prior to writing. Another advantage of using note cards is that they can be prepared and worked with in the library and then sorted into whatever order you require for later processing.

In Chapter 8 more detail is given about how to give citations in the text and write full bibliographic references, but suffice it to say that you must record full information on authors (including initials), titles, journal titles, publishers, year of publication, volume, issue and page numbers. Earlier we presented a citation to a magazine with an online link, the following two citations, one for a book and one for a journal article show the basic of what is needed for most material you will use.

Avgerou, C (2000) "Information systems: What sort of science is it?" *Omega: International Journal of Management Science*, Vol. 28, pp 567–579.

Bijker, W E (1995) *Of Bicycles, Bakelite, and Bulbs: Towards a Theory of Sociotechnical Change* Cambridge, Mass: MIT Press.

All other things being equal, the number of references is generally viewed positively. If you take ideas or phrases from a book or journal article, you must reference it. You certainly should not imagine that because you have a large number of references the examiners will conclude that you have not contributed anything yourself. In some cases, you may be making a contribution just by collecting the references together and summarizing what has been published in a given field – as is done in the survey articles discussed above.

Poor projects with a poor use of references tend to exhibit the following problems:

- There are no references, or just a few references to standard textbooks used in first year undergraduate courses. Given the increasing number of academic journals available online, a dearth of local library facilities is no longer a satisfactory excuse for the exclusive use of standard textbooks.
- There are a lot of references but they are all old and/or obscure. This suggests strongly to the examiners that these references have been merely copied from another article and that the student has not actually read the articles. There is no substitute for honesty and hard work! If you have not read a work, then think very hard before you put it in the references. There may be some legitimate reasons to do this – discussed below as secondary references – not many.
- The references in the text do not balance with the list at the back of the project. This again suggests, at worst, an element of plagiarism or, at best, a failure to recognise the importance of references.
- URLs swamp traditional sources. As we have noted above, most websites are commercial and are aimed at selling products. They are inherently biased and many are largely propaganda. There are some good sites that contain unbiased useful scientific information and these are worth citing, but you must give all web-based sources your own 'credibility check', including those of other universities and research centres.

Plagiarism

You search literature and read around your subject to gain information and ideas. You do not do it so as to find chunks of material that you can copy out into your project report. If you do copy out sections from a published work without clearly referencing it, you are guilty of plagiarism, which should be grounds for failing a course.

Plagiarism is to take the work of another person and use it as if it were one's own in such a way as to mislead the reader. Whole pieces of work can be plagiarised (for example, if a student put his or her name on another student's essay), or part pieces, where chapters or extracts may be lifted from other source, including the Internet, without acknowledgement

This definition is extracted from the University of Leicester statement on plagiarism included in student handbooks and the source is from the JISC web site devoted to plagiarism:

online.northumbria.ac.uk/faculties/art/information_studies/Imri/Jiscpas/site/jiscpas.asp

You may believe that such cheating is impossible to detect but examiners are surprisingly quick to detect changes in writing style, impossibly sophisticated or detailed arguments, or the use of unusual terminology. Examiners also have various online searching tools, from Google onward to check up on suspicious material. It is now quite common for universities to use specialised plagiarism detection sites as a standard part of assessment. One commercial site is www.turnitin.com, whereas in the UK the universities collectively have developed their own site and a detection service. You can visit this site at the URL given above, but given the length of the URL it may be better to search Google under 'JISC Plagiarism' – an example of *good* use of Google to find something you know exists. The site contains plenty of useful information for students, including information on how to avoid accusations of plagiarism and how to write within the conventions of academic study.

The message must be: **don't cheat, don't copy, do give appropriate citations and back them up with full references.**

As well as crediting the original author and signposting the development of your own ideas, citations and references are a way to provide supporting evidence for your own arguments or assumptions. Rather than assuming that it is common knowledge that, say, senior managers are worried about the financial returns from IT investments, a good supporting reference will add weight and authority to such a statement. For this reason, amongst others, it is essential to refer to the literature that you use at appropriate points in the text, and provide a full list of references at the end. This is far better than producing a lengthy unstructured bibliography disconnected from the text itself. It may be the case though that a separate bibliography or further reading section can be a valid part of a report, and serve to inform readers of additional useful works in the area or more general works consulted. In any event, references must be given in the appropriate format and the section on references in Chapter 9 gives further details on how references and citations should be written.

There is a particular problem when providing secondary references, that is when author A, whom you have read, cites author B, whom you have not. It may be allowable to cite such a reference, but it should be made plain that you have not read B's work, but have seen mention of it. For example, 'Avgerou and Cornford (1993), drawing on the work of Ackoff (1967), suggest that management information systems may mis-inform'.

A good use of references shows the examiners that you are familiar with the area that you are investigating. However, there is a danger of overkill; do not insert references solely for the sake of it. The inclusion of excessive references can make a work difficult to read and tends to break up the flow of ideas. In other words, up to a certain limit, you will be gaining marks for providing references; beyond that limit, you may find that you will begin to lose marks.

The literature review

A significant part of many projects will be a review of the literature in the area you study. You have to do this because otherwise you will not know what other people have done or said about your topic and be unable to use their insights and contributions. In research, to paraphrase the mathematician Isaac Newton, we see further when we stand on the shoulders of giants.

A review should consist of more than just a lengthy list of references or a sequence of précis of a random selection of papers. A good review is built up from a careful process of selecting and reading material, and analysing it for distinctive content. Webster and Watson (2002) provide a useful overview of one approach to preparing an literature review, based on a simple matrix of authors down one side, and key concepts or themes along the top. Of course the themes may shift a bit as you work, but in this way you can easily add more materials (more articles or books), and keep track of the developing picture. Table 6.1 below gives a simple example for some hypothetical new technology for business organizations.

By reading around a particular topic area in books and academic journals, you will soon notice that some items are cited repeatedly. These are usually core references and should be hunted down, read carefully and occupy prime positions in your review. In a fast-changing but complex area like information systems, you also need to be sensitive to the publication dates. However, don't fall into the trap of thinking that anything over five years old is automatically

Table 6.1 Simple literature review structure

Author	Date	Business benefits	Implementation approach	Model of organizational change	etc.
Smith	1997	Efficiency	Planned change	None	…
Jones	2001	Global reach	Socio-technical approach		…
Brown	2000	Competitive advantage	Emergent and evolutionary	Learning organization	…
…	…	…	…	…	

defunct – most areas have their 'timeless classics', old articles that remain highly relevant to this day. At the same time, you can easily make yourself look a little ridiculous by referring to 'recent' research (or data) that is more than ten years old. For example, Michael Porter's work on information technology and competitive advantage, published in 1985 may still be relevant to discussions on business strategy, but it is by no means 'recent' research (Porter and Millar, 1985).

Hart (1998, p. 53) provides a useful list of 'information components' that a reader should be expecting to extract when they read an academic source:

arguments	concepts	conclusions	definitions	ethics
events	evidence	hypothesis	interpretations	justifications
motives	perspectives	politics	problems	questions
standpoints	styles	techniques	theory	ways of thinking

The list is long and it is perhaps impossible to keep track of all these elements all the time, but almost any really useful paper will have some distinctive characteristics that can be described in some of these terms.

A good review should contain an account of how the literature of your topic area develops its themes and the key ideas introduced. It should also contain a requisite amount of creative criticism, in terms of pointing out limitations, inconsistencies or ambiguities. However, when you are writing a critical review, do not resort to satire, snide comments or libel. It is very easy, with the benefit of hindsight, to criticize the work of others and to believe that the most recent work provides the definitive insight. This is particularly true in the rapidly moving world of computers and information systems, but it is important to give credit to pioneers and to remember that many of the really important ideas that are used in the field are several years old or more.

A good literature review within a student project should act as a guide to the 'academic thinking' in your chosen field. 'Academic thinking' will include the theories and models used, the research approaches adopted, the concepts that are identified, and the empirical sites used for research. You should expect that there will be some progression or debate over time in your topic, so you will probably be telling a bit of history too. You will also need to make some judgement of the literature you are reviewing, is it essentially normative, explanatory or critical? Does it link together and create a sense of a cumulative research endeavour, or is it fragmented with different authors pursuing very different themes? You will probably want to say something about how successful research in your area has been – what new knowledge has been produced, and what controversies (arguments and counter arguments) have been raised?

By the end of a literature review a reader should be aware of the current state of knowledge and debate – what are the prevailing theoretical views, what lessons have been learned, how has this been reflected in professional practices, and what are the most interesting un-resolved questions? Finally, you will need to express the essential insights that you have gained from the literature. What is your preferred perspective/argument? Why? Where would you like to see further development of knowledge on this topic? What gap in the topic can you identify and how is your project going to add to the stock of knowledge in this area?

In this way a good literature review, even if it is less than 1000 words, sets the scene for the particular work you are doing and conveys to your reader a confident familiarity with the broad area and insight into how the field might be taken on further.

Summary

- To do good project work you need to carefully consider the sources of information that are available to you, and develop the skills needed to make the best of them.
- The literature of information systems is diverse; to access it will require careful work in libraries using the various computerized tools available. You should explore not only books but also journals and conference proceedings.
- Most projects will require some literature review to be written, structuring prior knowledge in the area and identifying gaps that you can contribute to filling.

Further reading

For undertaking a literature review Hart (1998) above gives an extended coverage and has many useful suggestions; the book is written from a strong social science perspective. Denscombe (2002) gives useful advice on writing a literature review, and is very clear as to its purpose. Creme and Lea (1997) also offers some useful guidance on how to read literature and how to take notes as you do so.

Creme, P. and M. R. Lea (1997) *Writing at University: A Guide for Students* (Buckingham England; Philadelphia: Open University Press).

Denscombe, M. (2002) *Ground Rules for Good Research: A 10 Point Guide for Social Researchers* (Buckingham: Open University Press).

Web resources

Google search engine www.google.com
The American Association for Computing Machinery www.acm.org
The American Institute for Electrical and Electronic Engineers Computer Society www.computer.org
The Association for Information Systems www.aisnet.org
CIO Magazine www.cio.com
ISWorld Net www.isworld.org
JISC Website online.northumbria.ac.uk/faculties/art/information_studies/Imri/Jiscpas/site/jiscpas.asp
See also www.turnitin.com

References

Ackoff, R. (1967) 'Management misinformation systems', Management Science, vol. 14, no. 4, pp. 133–36.

Alavi, M. and D. E. Leidner (2001) 'Review: Knowledge Management and Knowledge Management Systems: Conceptual Foundations and Research Issues', *MIS Quarterly*, vol. 25, pp. 107–36.

Dedrick, J., V. Gurbaxani and K. L. Kraemer (2003) 'Information Technology and Economic Performance: A Critical Review of the Empirical Evidence', *ACM Computing Surveys*, vol. 35, pp. 1–28.

Hart, C. (1998) *Doing a Literature Review* (Sage, London).

Ivory, M. I. and M. A. Hearst (2001) 'The State of the Art in Automating Usability Evaluation of User Interfaces', *ACM Computing Surveys*, vol. 33, pp. 470–516.

Mylonopoulos, N. A. and V. Theoharakis (2001) 'Global perceptions of IS journals', *Communications of the ACM*, vol. 44, no. 9, pp. 29–33.

Porter, M. and V. Millar (1985) 'How information technology can give you competitive advantage', *Harvard Business Review*, vol. 63, no. 4, pp. 149–60.

Robey, D., M.-C. Boudreau and G. M. Rose (2000) 'Information Technology and Organisational Learning: A Review and Assessment of Research', *Accounting, Management, and Information Technology*, vol. 10, pp. 125–55.

Schwartz, R. B. and M. C. Russo (2004) 'How to quickly find articles in the top IS journals', *Communications of the ACM*, vol. 47, no. 2, pp. 98–101.

Webster, J. and R. Watson (2002) 'Analyzing the Past to Prepare for the Future: Writing a Literature Review', *MIS Quarterly*, vol. 6, pp. xiv–xxiii.

Collecting research data

- **Questionnaires and surveys**
- **Good survey practice**
- **Interviews**
- **Documentation and text resources**
- **Observation**
- **Variety in data collection**

Researching and reading the academic and professional literature discussed in the previous chapter can provide sound foundation for a project, but almost all projects will then go on to undertake some data gathering from the world beyond the university – the so-called *real world*. This is what we refer to as empirical research, research that finds out from the world and provides experience that we can use to achieve better understanding of that world. Some projects will base their information gathering around the use of 'fact finding' or analysis techniques specific to information systems development, including techniques such as software engineering requirements determination, object oriented systems analysis or soft systems methodology. These areas are not discussed in detail in this book since it is assumed that those undertaking such projects are familiar with them, and should certainly make reference to more specialized texts. In this chapter, we discuss some of the techniques that may be less familiar or less formally understood including developing questionnaires and undertaking interviews.

Questionnaires and surveys

If part of a project depends upon carrying out a survey, perhaps considering the use of a particular new technology, for example a new technology such as personal digital assistants or PDAs, a new development technique such as the use of object oriented analysis, or some management practice such as post implementation evaluation, a questionnaire may be a suitable way to collect information from a range of relevant people. It is certainly one of the few data collection methods that allow a researcher to obtain views or data from a large number of organizations or individuals in a limited time period. If all goes well questionnaires will come back to you fully filled in and ready for analysis. Questionnaires can be distributed by post, by hand, by fax or e-mail, or placed on-line for completing over the Internet. There are a number of specialized software packages designed for preparing questionnaires for distribution over the Internet. Examples include SurveyMonkey, WebSurveyor and Zoomerang and it is worth investigating if your university or college has some such software available to you. You may also be able to develop your own online survey with basic web tools and some people have even done this with Excel. However, survey research does not always go so easily, and questionnaires do have a number of serious problems and constraints on their usage; so much so that students (and their advisers) should think very carefully whether they are worth the effort. Some of the main issues that need to be considered are listed in Box 7.1 below.

Most fundamentally, any questionnaire or survey is developed so as to provide answers to previously established questions. So there is a lot of work to be done before any survey is sent out to establish what questions to ask. Survey design thus follows on from some prior activity that establishes what the potentially relevant factors are, and how they can be measured; behind a good survey is some hypothesis or model of how the world works. For example, we may want to investigate the attitude to a new information system in a company and discover why some people have seen it as a success, while others have rejected it. What is our model – what factors do we think might be significant?

BOX 7.1

Key issues in considering survey research

- Effort required
- Developing a sampling frame
- Problems of poor response
- Problems of bias
- Limited to well understood topics
- Structure of questions
- Need to pilot

Is it based on the length of training given, the length of time spent in the organization, people's age, gender, educational background, the sign of the zodiac they were born under, or their shoe size? Some of these are more plausible than others, but we probably can't ask our respondents to answer all such questions. So, it is our job to build some prior model of the phenomena under study, drawing from the literature as discussed in the chapter earlier, and on this basis to start to prepare a questionnaire.

Effort

The effort and cost of designing, producing and distributing large numbers of questionnaires is considerable. You may have to go through three or four iterations before you reach a satisfactory design and, because of the problems of response rate, you will probably need to send out a large number of questionnaires in order to get sufficient responses to make any analysis worthwhile. You will also probably need to do some follow-up procedure to improve the rate of response or to understand who it is who is not responding. There is also the need to obtain and computerize a sizeable mailing list, as well as to enter data once it is returned.

Response

For most questionnaires sent at random to people in business or organizations, a response rate of 20 per cent should be seen as quite a good response. Poorly designed questionnaires may only produce a 10 per cent response or even less. The rate is likely to be higher in more restricted circumstances; for example, for questionnaires distributed internally to an organization's workforce, with full management support. This implies that many surveys are not going to achieve results that have formal statistical significance.

Bias

The response, as well as being small, is likely to be from a biased sample. Usually the enthusiasts (for a particular technology or technique) will predominate, as those with less enthusiasm may not be motivated enough to complete the questionnaire. Thus, you cannot normally assume that the responses are representative of the whole population. Particular organizational or national cultures and values may determine the response rate; for example some organizations have an explicit policy that they do not respond under any circumstances, while others may worry that their responses will become known to their competitors.

Well understood topics

Questionnaires are suitable for only certain fairly straightforward topics; you cannot expect respondents to answer questions on highly abstract, complex or poorly understood topics. People do not like to display their confusion or lack of knowledge, so that even if you provide a contact telephone number for assistance with the questionnaire, they will not use it. There is thus usually no way that you can add any further explanation or clarification to the brief instructions that are on the questionnaire itself.

Focus of questions

A poor choice of question types can negate the responses. Open questions, where you just provide a blank space and expect the respondent to fill in, say, her views of the advantages of a particular technology, may be too demanding of respondents' time and creative effort. On the other hand, closed (or multiple choice) questions may be too restrictive or may offer inappropriate options with your respondent feeling that really none of the options offered apply to them.

Design

It is surprisingly difficult to formulate questions that are:

- clear, unambiguous and easy for respondents to understand;
- free of unnecessary assumptions;
- free of jargon;
- comprehensive (in that they cover any possible case);
- answerable directly without respondents having to seek out information themselves.

For questions that require a graded response (e.g. 'strongly disagree', 'disagree', etc.) it is often difficult to select scales that are meaningful for the respondent as well as providing useful data for analysis. In any case, before you prepare a survey you should have thought through the basic analysis you intend to do, and thereby cross checked you questions to avoid inconsistencies.

If at all possible, previous questionnaires that address the same issues should be consulted. They may be printed along with articles reporting previous research in the area, or they may be available on request from people who have undertaken such research. The ISWorld Net site (http://www.isworld.org/surveyinstruments/surveyinstruments.htm) contains much information on survey research as well as a repository of old questionnaires (called instruments to reflect their role as a scientific instrument) and references to the published papers that have used them, precisely so that other researchers can reuse them. Indeed, it is sound practice if possible to reuse an old questionnaire or some questions drawn from it. This allows a comparison of new results with old and helps to build up the credibility of your own work. See for example Cornford and Doukidis (1991) in which questions from an earlier survey were used to validate the response in a new survey. A classic example of such a survey instrument is the one used by Davis (1989) in his paper *Perceived usefulness, perceived ease of use, and user acceptance*, based on a model known as the Technology Acceptance Model (TAM). You can find the instrument used on the ISWorld site. This provides quite a short set of questions, 6 for usefulness and 6 for ease of use each based on a 7 point Lickert scale – examples of each are shown below in Table 7.1. Note that 6 questions are needed to create a balanced version of each construct (usefulness, ease of use) – it is not appropriate to just ask if software is useful, rather you want to ask questions about things like helping with the task at hand, increasing productivity, making the job easier.

Respondent bias

You may be tempted to ask for respondents' views on matters that impinge on their status or prestige or that of their organization. For example, the question 'Does your organization use IT strategically?' may elicit a large proportion

Table 7.1 Excerpt from measurement scales for perceived usefulness and perceived easy of use (Davis, 1989)

Perceived usefulness
Using *this software* in my job would enable me to accomplish tasks more quickly
    Likely   *Unlikely*
        extremely – quite – slightly – neither – slightly – quite – extremely

Perceived ease of use
               Learning to use *this software* would be easy for me
    Likely   *Unlikely*
        extremely – quite – slightly – neither – slightly – quite – extremely

---

of erroneous affirmative answers because the respondents believe that this will give a good impression to the researcher. This is known as the *well, they would say that, wouldn't they* problem.

Thus, through misunderstanding, or lack of information (or occasionally malicious intent), respondents may provide inaccurate replies. These are then fed through to the analysis, producing inaccurate conclusions.

The need to pilot

It is usually essential to carry out one or more pilot runs with any questionnaire, to ensure that the questions are understandable. The pilot can be tested with some firms or individuals with whom you are on particularly good terms, or with your friends. However, you must remember that the purpose of the pilot is to identify ambiguities and other problems with the questions, so whoever is involved in this must be willing to give critical responses. This stage should be taken seriously – a fumbled pilot may allow serious errors to slip through the net which can significantly compromise the data collected from the final version of a questionnaire. Remember too that such things as spelling mistakes or wonky layout on the page in a survey make a very bad impression, so many checks are needed to protect against such things happening.

Good survey practice

The experience of researchers suggests that it is most appropriate to use questionnaires for investigating currently topical subjects where people want to contribute to the discussion or will have well formed opinions. Researchers need to be careful in compiling a mailing list. Rather than sending questionnaires to the IT managers of the top 200 companies (who are typically bombarded by questionnaires) select medium-sized companies or concentrate on a particular industrial sector. The latter strategy will enable you to tailor the questions to that sector and perhaps get more comparable results. You should also use up-to-date sources for compiling a mailing list.

Ideally, a questionnaire should be addressed to either a named individual or a particular job function, for example the information systems manager. It is also good practice to give respondents a deadline for return of the completed questionnaires, but this should be realistic. The deadline should neither be too soon, nor too far off; a reasonable time would be three weeks from the date of distribution. Following up non-respondents by telephone after the deadline can be effective, although time consuming. Response may improve if you have the added authority (and letter heading) of a trade association or other body.

The covering letter that you enclose with a survey is important; it should be well written and should be aimed at motivating potential respondents to complete the questionnaire. Thus it should politely explain the purpose of the study and appeal to them either as contributors of important data or as experts in the field. You may even wish to offer the respondents a copy of your final report, but if you make the offer then be sure to carry it through. It is also good practice to enclose a self-addressed envelope; a relatively official address (e.g. your university or college) looks more impressive. The envelope need not be stamped as most organizations can do this simply but they may object to the trouble of typing out your address on an envelope. A self-addressed envelope also should ensure that responses actually find you.

Pay attention to questionnaire structure and the ordering of questions. This should be systematic and logical; people do not normally respond well to 'random walks'. Try to make the layout of the questionnaire attractive, so that respondents can almost enjoy completing it; for example make sure that you line up response boxes and provide clear instructions as to how to complete the questionnaire.

You should of course avoid questions that are unanswerable (e.g. people do not normally know the exact turnover of the organization), unnecessary (e.g. do not ask for the respondent's educational background unless you *really* need it) or insult the intelligence (e.g. providing unnecessary instructions). Try not to make the questionnaire too long – three to four pages are a good target. You should also show through the questions that you already have a good understanding of the topic and that you are keen to receive 'expert' views. Be careful too regarding issues of security or confidentiality – you cannot normally expect respondents to provide you with sensitive information. In any case, wherever possible, provide the respondent with the opportunity to submit the questionnaire anonymously. Most of these hints apply as much to 'internal' questionnaires, where you are surveying the workforce of a company, as to external questionnaires.

Designing a questionnaire that potential respondents will be motivated to complete, but which will still provide you with useful data, is a difficult task that should not be approached lightly. If you do decide to use a questionnaire, then you should seek some expert advice or read a specialized text such as Gillham (2000) or Moser and Kalton (1971).

Because of the inherent problems with questionnaires, they are often best supported with at least a few interviews. So, to end on a more positive note, questionnaires, as well as providing useful data, can also give you potential interviewees if, as one of the questions, you ask respondents whether they would be prepared to be interviewed. This can provide a good source of interviewees, without the time and effort attached to cold telephone calls.

Interviews

An alternative, or complement, to questionnaires and surveys is to interview respondents in person to collect research data. The strengths of interviews can be seen in areas where questionnaires are relatively weak. Thus, interviews offer the chance to explore topics in depth and to gain an appreciation of the organizational context within which the interviewee is addressing the topic. Interviews allow for interaction between the interviewer and the interviewee, so that where there is any ambiguity or misunderstanding, each party can provide further explanation or clarification. Interviews also allow you to adjust your line of questioning depending on the interviewee's responses; for example, expanding on areas of interest and cutting back areas that are clearly irrelevant. In this way interviews can deal with much more complex topics than questionnaires and deal with topics for which different people may have very different perspectives.

Interviews are usually classified in terms of the amount of underlying structure that the researcher imposes on them. These range from the totally unstructured interview, where the interviewer merely provides the topic and the conversation proceeds without any planning, to the totally structured, where the interviewer asks only pre-prepared questions in a pre-planned sequence, without divergence and with the minimum of explanation. This kind of interview may also be based on the completion of a questionnaire. Both extremes of interview format have their particular uses but also their dangers, in terms of lack of completeness or failing to reap the benefits of the personal interview. This means that either extreme is unlikely to be suitable for the sort of study that student-researchers are involved in, and the compromise position, the semi-structured interview, will most often be chosen. In this approach the interviewer prepares an outline for the interview in advance, including a number of key questions, to act as a guide, though without the intention of following it rigorously. This will ensure that the same topics are covered in each interview, but the emphasis can be shifted as appropriate.

BOX 7.2

Critical interview problems

- Getting to see people
- Getting to see the right people
- Time to prepare, travel and *most important* to write-up
- Keeping interviews on the topic

Just as with a survey and discussed earlier, this does imply that the researcher has done some prior work to develop clear ideas about what topics should be addressed in the interview, and in what sequence and with what priority.

Despite the advantages of interviewing, and even assuming that you have adequately prepared for the interview, there are still a number of potential problems as shown in Box 7.2.

Getting to people

Many people, especially busy managers, may decline to be interviewed, either because they do not have the time or else because they do not see any apparent gains from an interview. Acceptance can often be facilitated by approaching the person carefully (see below) or using your own, or your adviser's, contacts or influence. It may be that an interview can be held over the phone, but it will have to be brief and very much to the point.

A variant of the problem of getting to people is getting to the wrong people. It can be very frustrating to find that you are interviewing the wrong person and that he or she is either not involved with the topic or lacks experience or seniority to give an informed opinion. In this case, it may be best to cut short the interview politely and ask whether the interviewee could help you obtain an interview with someone more knowledgeable.

Sticking to a topic

Some interviewees may not fully understand what information you require and, as a result, the interview rambles off into the realms of the irrelevant. It can be very difficult to redirect the conversation back to your intended area, especially when the interviewee is a senior manager. Nonetheless you have to take control and try, politely, to return to the issues of concern to you.

When preparing such a semi-structured interview, think carefully about the types of question you will ask. Some examples might include the following – for more information see chapter 3 of Bauer and Gaskell (2000):

Could you tell me about ...
How would you describe ...
When did you first start to ...
What sort of a business might want to ...
I don't understand why, could you tell me a bit more. ...
Is there anything else (or anyone else) which I should know about ...

Often, especially with busy managers, the interview is subject to constant interruptions, from either telephone calls or other visitors. This can be annoying, although it should be remembered that managers may be quite accustomed to such an environment and will not necessarily lose their train of thought.

Effort required

Research based on interviews can be surprisingly time consuming; in addition to the preparation and the interview itself, there is also travelling time, waiting time and the time spent writing up and analysing the responses. If the interview method is chosen as the primary means of collecting data, then it is important that the process is taken seriously and time is devoted to it. It can seem to some students that interviews are the 'easy option', a few conversations and the main body of the research is done. This is certainly not true. Interviews are a valuable research tool, but they are no short cut to results.

Good interview practice

The hints given above for questionnaires may also be relevant to interviews. In addition, the following suggestions may be useful in arranging and conducting interviews, so that you can get the most from the investment of time and effort.

It is important to be polite and business like in both arranging and conducting the interview. Try to arrange it well in advance and give the interviewee as much choice as possible regarding dates and times. When you ask for the interview, you should explain the objectives of the study and the sort of information that you would like the interviewee to provide. This lessens the chances that you will interview the wrong person and allows the interviewee to reflect on the topic and prepare any relevant data. On the day, dress respectably and arrive punctually. If a telephone call or visitor interrupts you during the interview you should offer to leave the room.

As with questionnaires, you should prepare your questions carefully but you should consider taking advantage of the interview situation by asking different types of questions; for example, you could ask an interviewee to tell you how they dealt with a particularly difficult problem or transaction (the critical incident approach) or, try to encourage other forms of story telling. Questions may need to be a little challenging to elicit a strong response, but you should never be rude or try to tell an interviewee where they are going wrong. They may have used rather strange procedures or have odd notions, but there may be a good reason for their position. Remember that an interviewee probably has more experience than a researcher of solving the particular problems of their organization.

You should pay careful attention to the timing and structure of the interview. Most people will not be able to give you more than an hour of their time. Do not spend too long at the start of the interview collecting background data and pushing the interesting and important questions to the end; bored interviewees rarely provide good responses and you may run out of time anyway. On occasion, you may be pleasantly surprised by the amount of time and attention that is given to you by the interviewee. However, to ensure that they do not in retrospect regret the time spent with you, it is a good idea to remind them of the time once the allotted period is over.

Sometimes it is useful to tape-record an interview, but you must ask the interviewee's permission first and turn off the tape recorder if requested at any point. Even if you do record an interview, you should also make outline notes yourself in order to keep track of the interview and just in case the tape-recorder is malfunctioning. Furthermore, transcribing recorded conversations is a very tedious and time-consuming task. For the scale of project that this book discusses, recordings, if they are made, are probably best used for checking back to clarify responses and for filling in points that you missed first time around, rather than as the basis for full transcripts.

Before attending an interview consider how you intend to manage the interview closure. Do not forget to thank your interviewee for their time and assistance. At the same time, it can be useful at this point to ask whether you might approach them again if you find later that some aspect of what is discussed is unclear. As soon as possible after the interview you should write up your account. When ever possible this should be on the same day and certainly before the next batch of interviews. If a number of interviews are held, and the writing up is delayed, then it will become very much more difficult to disentangle the separate events.

Documentation and text resources

It is often useful to study relevant documentation either as the main basis for a project or as a complement to other methods of data collection. For example, if you are studying the impact of a technology on people's jobs, it may be instructive to look at their written job descriptions before and after the implementation of the technology. This is very much part of the 'formal system' and may not be followed in practice but it is still part of the 'story'. Similarly, external (consultancy) reports on the financial or business health of companies that you are studying can be useful. If you are studying some aspect of the public sector, say computers in healthcare, then government reports, debates in parliament or speeches by ministers might provide useful data that is worthy of its own careful analysis.

In large organizations any IS project management structures will probably result in many documents and minutes of meetings. If you can have access to these, then this can provide a very useful source of data, in particular as a means of discovering what was said or done some time ago. Thus it may be interesting to contrast what interviewees say about events 3 years ago, and contrast it with the formal record of the meeting minutes.

Observation

We should also not forget observation. By merely keeping your eyes open, you will get a 'feel' as to whether the organization and its staff are busy or sitting around doing nothing, whether the work environment is well-ordered or chaotic and so on. Because of, say, the poor layout of the offices, you may find it difficult to find a particular office. Your interviewees may appear stressed or relaxed. All of these visual clues may indicate something unsaid but relevant. Building on the sociological technique of participant observation you might be able to develop good data resources by working within the field that you seek to study. For example, a study of computer use by pupils in a school or nurses in a hospital, could be largely based on such an approach if you have an opportunity to work within such a community. We would however empha-size that this means more than 'hanging around' and writing up what you think is going on. You need to keep meticulous research notes, be very sharp in your observation of what is going on, and provide a relevant analytical framework to structure the findings.

Flick (2002) suggests that observational studies will probably go through three stages. First *descriptive observation* to provide orientation and to capture the complexity of what is going on. Then comes *focused observation*, moving to a particular concern with observing selected aspects of what happens that are relevant to the research question. Finally, comes *selective observation*, in which the researcher actively seeks out examples of some particular activity or event that has been highlighted through the previous stages.

Variety in data collection

In this chapter we have considered the two most common data collection meth-ods used in the field of information systems: surveys and interviewing as well as briefly considering the use of documentation and observation. It should be clear that there are many other possibilities for collecting data that may be appropri-ate in particular situations. For example, research may be based on asking people to keep diaries of their activities or on 'computer collected' data, such as usage statistics drawn from an electronic mail system or discussions within an online bulletin board. We have also not considered collecting data under experimental conditions, for example testing alternative user interface designs by using fellow students as the research guinea pigs. The intention of this chapter is not to promote the particular methods discussed here over any others. Each project will require that appropriate means of data collection be identified and evaluated before any particular research approach is adopted. However, the topics discussed here should provide a useful starting point in considering the implications of any particular chosen methods for data collection.

Summary

- Surveys can provide valuable data, but demand careful preparation and must be based on a clear model prior to their development.
- Interviews allow you to gather richer and more contextual information, but equally you need to do prior work and control the process.
- Documentary resources may provide the central data source for a project, but more often provide a useful complement to other sources.
- Observation, either participant or non-participant, can be a powerful means to get inside a research situation, but as with the other techniques, do demand careful preparation and meticulous attention.

Further reading

Bell (1999) gives a useful brief chapter on interviews. For a more theoretical discussion of interviews within the qualitative research tradition, see Silverman (1993). Gaskell's (2000) chapter on interviewing provides a lot of relevant suggestions and good advice and is well complimented by the relevant chapter in Flick (2002).

Bell, J. (1999) *Doing your Research Project: A Guide for First-time Researchers in Education and Social Science* (Milton Keynes: Open University Press).

Silverman, D. (1993) *Interpreting Qualitative Data: Methods for Analysing Talk, Text and Interaction* (London: Sage).

Web resources

ISWorldNet www.isworld.org/surveyinstruments/surveyinstruments.htm

References

Cornford, T. and G. Doukidis (1991) 'An investigation into the use of computers within operational research', *European Journal of Information Systems*, vol. 1, no. 2, pp. 131–40.

Davis, F. D. (1989) 'Perceived usefulness, perceived ease of use, and user acceptance', *MIS Quarterly*, vol. 13, no. 3, pp. 319–40.

Flick, U. (2002) *An Introduction to Qualitative Research* (London: Sage).

Gaskell, G. (2000) 'Individual and group interviewing', in M. Bauer and G. Gaskell (eds) (2000) *Qualitative Researching with Text, Image and Sound: A Practical Handbook* (London: Sage).

Gillham, B. (2000) *Developing a Questionnaire* (London: Continuum).

Moser, C. A. and G. Kalton (1971) *Survey Methods in Social Investigation* (London: Gower).

Analysing research data

- **Quantitative analysis**
- **Preparing the data**
- **Presenting the data**
- **Drawing inferences**
- **Interpreting the results**
- **Case studies and qualitative analysis**
- **Sequential analysis**
- **Interpretation**
- **Testing**
- **Presentation**
- **Combining quantitative and qualitative analysis**

Many information systems projects have a significant empirical element and, for this reason, students spend considerable time and effort collecting data by means such as postal questionnaires, interviews or involvement in case studies. Having collected large amounts of data, much of which may seem interesting, confusing or downright obvious, the students then have to decide how to use this data to develop and support their arguments. This analysis task is the subject of this chapter.

Our experience suggests that, for a variety of reasons, data analysis is often carried out rather badly with the result that much of the valuable data collected with great effort goes to waste. Either students shy away from any analysis, leaving the reader wondering frustratedly what could have been achieved or, at the other extreme, students bombard the reader with endless tables, long quotes and sophisticated statistics so that the key points of the argument are swamped.

The aim of this chapter is to provide some general guidelines to help information systems students approach the process of data analysis and avoid the most common mistakes. Space does not permit anything like a complete treatment of this topic and this chapter is no substitute for a good specialist textbook, a number of which are mentioned later. In terms of quantitative analysis, our intention is to provide the non-statisticians with a basic route-map to find their way around the maze of complex statistical techniques and terminology. However, there is a lot more to data analysis than mere statistics, and the growing popularity of case studies and of interpretivist approaches means that an overview of qualitative analysis techniques is also required. For each approach our stance is a pragmatic one of helping the reader to select appropriate tools for the job in hand.

Although unpopular, statistics are hard to avoid, as much of the data from information systems research projects concerns multiple cases, originating from questionnaires or large-scale interviews. We believe that problems with the employment of statistical techniques should be met head-on. In addition, much of the current information systems research makes considerable use of relatively sophisticated statistics and students should at least have an under-standing of the benefits and drawbacks of this approach.

This chapter is accordingly divided into two main parts: quantitative and qualitative analysis. The discussion of quantitative analysis begins with a brief examination of the role of statistical techniques within information systems research projects. We then provide a description of each of the four key processes within quantitative analysis: preparing the data, presenting the data, drawing inferences and interpreting the results. The second part of the chapter is con-cerned with qualitative analysis, and examines the main characteristics of qualitative data before following a similar process-oriented structure.

Quantitative analysis

The use of statistical techniques in IS research

Statistics is a field surrounded by a certain mystique which, ironically enough, is analogous to that associated with computing and information technology. Like IT, it is a field that is conceptually fairly straightforward but there are enough, highly visible, complications that tend to scare away the non-numerate of a nervous disposition. This may be partly because of the way statistics has traditionally been taught in universities, where purists have tended to empha-size the mathematical roots rather than the practical applications. The end result is typically that generations of students struggle through statistics examinations solely on the basis of rote learning and good luck. Later, these students are lost when it comes to dealing with real problems that require a statistical solution. There is also evidence of poor usage of statistical analysis within the information systems literature (Baroudi and Orlikowski, 1989).

In trying to strip away the mystique, our first task is to discuss 'what' we are trying to do with these techniques and 'why'. The student who has collected vast amounts of data needs statistical tools and techniques in order to summarize the data and present it in a readable form, which is the field known as descriptive statistics, and then to try to extract some sort of meaning or relationships between the different items of data, the field known as inferential statistics. The aim of the student is to 'tell a story', 'paint a picture' or demonstrate the validity of an argument and, properly used, statistical techniques are an excellent aid in this endeavour.

The next point to note is that statistics is very much a general purpose discipline, providing tools appropriate for a wide range of disciplines from physics and the natural sciences to medicine and engineering, as well as to such social sciences as economics, sociology and anthropology. We have argued strongly that information systems are social systems and thus the part of the statistical toolbox that concerns us is mostly the set of tools for social sciences (see Healey, 2002). It is unfortunate that many introductory statistics courses focus on the mathematically tidier context of continuous variables, more often found in the natural sciences.

Statistical software packages

For any data analysis of any size at all, the use of statistical software packages is essential. Well-established packages, such as SPSS, are widely available in colleges and universities. Although most of these packages originated in a mainframe environment, from where they offered a particularly unfriendly interface to naive users and non-statisticians; their MS-Windows implementations are much easier to use and, for any significant analysis, they should be the tool of choice. Normally they are preferable to PC spreadsheet software (such as Excel) which typically does not have all the statistical functions needed. Such statistical packages should be within the grasp of most serious information systems students. They offer a wide range of statistical tools such as regression, analysis of variance, non-parametric statistics, cluster analysis, factor analysis and multi-dimensional scaling, as well as the ability to produce various types of scatterplots, histograms and pie charts.

This wide-ranging functionality can be quite disconcerting and unwieldy for non-statisticians wishing to carry out very basic analysis. However, two factors in favour of the specialist packages are that, first, the functionality is available should it be required later in the analysis, and, second, many years

---

BOX 8.1

Golden rules of data preparation

- Time spent on data preparation is time well spent
- Remove all manifestly misleading responses
- Categorization and coding must be comprehensible and consistent
- Preserve original data, coding sheets and the coding schema
- Design worksheets, do not just let them happen

---

of experience with specialist packages have meant that most universities offer short courses, additional documentation and comprehensive help-desk facilities for novices. Clearly, students should select their package based on the needs of the situation in hand.

The final point that must be emphasized is that students must have a good understanding of both the statistical tools and the data *before* they start plugging away at the software. This software is not designed to teach basic statistics and the unwary who venture into detailed analysis without an understanding of the basic processes will almost certainly end up with piles of meaningless statistics.

Preparing the data

This, the first stage of data analysis, is concerned with transforming the raw data into a form suitable for presentation and statistical analysis. Time spent on this stage is nearly always time well spent as there is nothing worse than having to repeat an entire analysis due to a belated realization that the underlying data is suspect in some way. For the sake of clarity, in this and the following sections, we shall assume that the data is in the form of returned postal questionnaires; the treatment of similar interview and observational data should follow the same procedure (see Box 8.1).

Cleaning and coding the data

First, the returned questionnaires should be read through to see how the respondents interpreted and answered the questions. Despite pilot experiments and close proof-reading, ambiguous questions slip through into the final questionnaire with depressing regularity. Such erroneous responses should be removed, together with any obvious inconsistencies; for example, computers were first introduced into the organization in 1807. Other non-usable responses include questionnaires where virtually every question is answered by 'N/A'.

This initial scan of the data may also reveal certain questions or whole questionnaires that are clearly outliers because the responses differ so much from the norm. In cases such as the multi-billion dollar corporation that appears in a survey of small businesses, it is clear that the whole questionnaire should be withdrawn but, in most cases, the treatment of outliers depends on the situation/question. Similarly, the treatment of 'don't know' (and other null) responses is situation dependent: in some cases, the few such responses could be mentioned in a footnote while, in others, a large number might merit a separate analysis. Other 'data cleaning' operations might include standardizing the units or number of decimal places for quantitative data.

Having cleaned the data, the next stage is to prepare it for analysis which, in most cases, means to prepare it for entry into a software package. For a number of pragmatic reasons: conciseness, the need for categorization and the demands of the statistical software, this means coding the data with a numerical code.

Such coding should be easy to remember/recognize; that is, it should be simple, logical and consistent. Thus, coding schemas such as the following are normally appropriate:

Very satisfied   = 4
Satisfied   = 3
Dissatisfied   = 2
Very dissatisfied = 1

Once the coding schema has been designed, this type of coding is clearly a straightforward way of coding simple semi-quantitative responses. Similarly, Likert scales lend themselves to direct coding. However, to avoid confusing or misleading results during statistical analysis, such schemas, especially regarding the application of low–high scales, should be applied to the data consistently throughout all the data; for example, 'yes' should always be '1' and 'no' always '0'.

Not all coding is necessarily this straightforward or mechanical. Some coding involves allocating responses to categories; for example, size of organization may be usefully represented by 'small', 'medium' and 'large', based on the number of employees. Thus, rather than entering the exact number of employees, the response is categorized and coded. Another example of categorization is the treatment sometimes given to the answers to open questions, which can be categorized according to the question.

Categorization as part of coding is not trivial and care needs to be given to the categories chosen. Above all, categorization needs to be meaningful from the perspective of the data. While it may be satisfying mathematically to show the information in deciles or centiles throughout, too many sparsely filled or over-full categories may obscure the picture. On the other hand, students should not 'fiddle' the categories in order to produce attractive but invalid results. Furthermore, students should retain a way of retrieving the raw data in case re-categorization is required when a better classification schema suggests itself later in the analysis. It is clearly sensible not to dispose of any data irrevocably but the level of refinement of data input to the software can be a difficult design decision.

Worksheet design

The next stage is to design the statistical worksheet that will form the computer's repository for the data. Statistical software uses worksheets (spreadsheets) which are huge tables allowing data to be stored in numerical form in rows and columns. Normally each case (respondent) forms a row and each question (or sub-question) a column. The rows normally present no problems as it is relatively clear how to delineate a case or respondent.

Organizing the columns can be more difficult as each cell can only take one figure. Thus each question (and sub-question) normally requires its own column and this has to be specified in advance. In addition, extra columns may be required for merging categories and other manipulations. Earlier PC software packages had a restricted number of columns available, necessitating the use of a second worksheet, but this is not usually a problem with today's software. Nevertheless, some form of estimation of the size of worksheet required for the analysis is a good first step.

The case of sub-questions concerns questions from the questionnaire where the respondent has to tick boxes indicating, say, the presence of a problem or benefit. For example:

Problems of ERP (enterprise resource planning) software
Technical   [ ]
Managerial   [ ]
Organizational   [ ]

Each of these aspects (e.g. technical) will require its own column which will be coded as either 'yes' or 'no'.

Care should be taken regarding the labelling of rows and columns so that each is clearly and unambiguously identified. For column headings, this is not as easy as it may appear, because often only short titles are permitted and many similar columns are often involved in an analysis.

Presenting the data

The second stage of data analysis is normally the selection of relevant and interesting sets of data from the huge amount stored in the worksheet to include in the student's 'Findings' chapter. This involves the selection and representation of the basic data in a concise but understandable fashion. It also involves the careful consideration of the content of tables and charts before considering their design aspects, which we discuss in Chapter 9.

Frequency distributions

The usual way of presenting summaries of a large amount of, basically, quantitative data is through frequency distributions, either in the form of tables or charts. These typically show the number or proportion of respondents who gave particular answers or values to a specific question.

Before discussing how to present tables and charts, one key point needs to be emphasized. The data collected normally represents a particular aspect of a complex social and organizational 'reality' (e.g. the disadvantages of ERP systems) in which the student is deeply interested, having worked with the data for many weeks. Normally sufficient data has been collected such that a table or graph can be produced for each of the questions on the questionnaire, which could number up to 50. Each of these questions could have some attendant complexity. However, the reader/adviser is normally less interested in the volume and complexity of the data and is looking for the student's ability to summarize this complex reality.

One way of summarizing data is to present averages for responses to particular questions. Depending upon the data concerned, these could take the form of the arithmetic mean or the median value of the responses. Purists would argue that one should not use the arithmetic mean for non-continuous, ordinal (see below) data such as Likert scales. However, we feel that it can be helpful, depending upon the circumstances and provided that care is taken with any further manipulations. Again, depending upon the circumstances, it may be relevant to illustrate the spread of the responses around the average using, for example, the standard deviation or the variance of the responses. The test for inclusion of this sort of information is: does it serve any purpose?

BOX 8.2

Golden rules of data description

- ■ 'Keep It Simple Stupid', but do not lose the meaning
- ■ Try to 'paint a picture' that summarizes and clarifies the key points to the reader, rather than emphasizing the complexity
- ■ Avoid duplication by integrating textual description, tables and graphs
- ■ More complex material and supplementary work should be placed in an appendix

---

Therefore, the message is *KISS – Keep It Simple, Stupid*. First, the number of tables presented in the main part of the final report should be kept to a minimum. This can be achieved first by avoiding tables for very simple data, such as 'yes or no' answers. For example, there is no need to produce a table to indicate that 70 per cent of the respondents believed that ERP systems are important and 30 per cent did not – this can be mentioned in the text. The second technique is to place peripheral data (e.g. the job title of the respondent) in an appendix, to which only the really interested reader needs to refer. However, care should be taken not to consign key tables and charts to an appendix. There is nothing more annoying for the reader than to have to keep referring to an appendix to make sense of the main text.

Similarly, it is important when writing up the description of the data to try to do so in an interesting way (see Box 8.2). Do not just repeat in your text the content of any tables or charts but also do not just present endless tables without any complementary text. Also, do not normally duplicate charts with tables. For some data, a chart may be preferable but if there is any doubt about reading the exact values, include a table in an appendix for support. Rather, the text should highlight the key results: the high and low values and any surprises.

Wherever appropriate, it is useful to intersperse quotes from the respondents amongst the tables and descriptive text. Such quotes may come from open questions in a postal survey or through interviews. Many such quotes may be of little value, but one often finds that a respondent who has been facing a particular problem in practice for some time is able to put it into words in an interesting fashion (often quite colourfully):

Working with end-users has broadened my outlook considerably but reduced my life expectancy by ten years. (Anonymous systems analyst)

Drawing inferences

In many cases, the purpose of empirical research is not just to describe what is happening in a particular area but rather to find evidence to support (or reject) certain ideas or theories. Thus, rather than just presenting the data, we are looking for conclusive evidence of relationships between particular sets of data, or evidence of a lack of a relationship. For example, we may believe that larger firms implemented ERP systems before smaller firms. Thus, we need to compare the answers to the 'firm size' and 'age of ERP system' questions and decide whether there is any difference between the two sets of data.

This area, known as inferential statistics, is a minefield for the unwary. It is all too easy to apply half-remembered statistical techniques to the wrong sort of data, resulting in a half-baked conclusion. On the other hand, properly applied statistical techniques can provide the key link between a mass of data and the ideas and arguments of the student. Space does not permit anything like a full discussion of the problems and opportunities here, and readers are referred to Healey (2002) for an excellent, highly accessible treatment of a tricky area.

Hypothesis generation and testing

In looking for relationships, we are typically looking for differences according to particular hypotheses (or ideas or theories) that we had at the research design stage. A hypothesis is a declared statement of the relationship between two or more variables, in general derived from some theory. Indeed, the questionnaire (or other research instrument) should have been designed to collect data that would help to indicate whether a particular relationship exists. At this design stage, we should have explicitly stated such hypotheses as part of the objectives of the research. However, often, perhaps halfway through the study, other hypotheses occur to us, perhaps on the basis of further reading, interviews or from studying the data collected. Nevertheless, from some source or other we should have a set of hypotheses concerning particular relationships. In statistical terms, hypotheses typically come in pairs: H_1 a particular relationship holds and H_0 the relationship does not hold (the null hypothesis).

Deciding which data to test

When confronted with large amounts of data, students should resist the temptation to start trying to correlate everything against everything else. There is an old saying in social science circles that 'Everything is correlated against everything else at the level of 0.3.' In other words, students should only test for associations which may be meaningful; for example, it is almost certainly pointless testing for an association between the size of the firm and the age of the respondent (unless this is the topic of the research). The discovery of spurious relationships can lead to wasting a lot of time and ingenuity trying unsuccessfully to explain them.

The first source of tests should be the research objectives themselves. If the data was collected to investigate certain relationships, then these relationships should be tested. It may be that there is no evidence of these relationships, but even a 'null result' is often a result. Students should then discuss why they could find no evidence of the proposed relationship.

However, it often happens that, in collecting the data, the student stumbles across an unexpected relationship through chance (otherwise known as serendipity). In other words, students should never be constrained by the original research objectives. The best way of finding such prizes is to study the data carefully; that is, to 'eyeball' the results. Whilst the use of statistical tables is essential for deciding whether a potential association is statistically significant, students should also examine the way the data looks. Adding equal measures of curiosity and intuition, even the inexperienced human eye is surprisingly good at spotting potential relationships. This can be facilitated by changing the form of the data a little. For example, rather than rushing into a regression analysis, the student could easily use the software to produce a quick scatterplot between two variables. The naked eye is surprisingly efficient at distinguishing possible relationships or suspicious clusters of datapoints. An alternative is to cross-tabulate the variables which may again reveal interesting patterns.

Cross-tabulations

In searching for relationships between two variables, a common technique is that of cross-tabulation (also known as contingency tables). This involves producing a simple table to show how one variable is distributed with relation to the other. For example, the degree of satisfaction with ERP software against whether the ERP support centre is a local one or is centralized at headquarters. It is traditional to put the independent variable along the top (columns) and the dependent one along the side (rows). In our case, the location of the ERP support centre is the independent variable and so we will place it along the top (Table 8.1). Most statistical software will produce a table like this very easily.

We should then inspect the data to see whether the percentages for each category of the independent variable are different within the categories of the

Table 8.1 Example of cross-tabulation

	ERP support centre		
	Local	HQ	Total
Very satisfied	6	2	8
Quite satisfied	10	6	16
Quite dissatisfied	5	5	10
Very dissatisfied	0	4	4
Total	21	17	38

dependent variable. Reading across the rows of Table 8.1, there seems to be a tendency for the local support centres to produce satisfaction more often than the headquarters ones. We need to see whether the larger numbers are situated on a diagonal; this is easier to see in a two-by-two table. We should then try to determine whether there is a statistically significant relationship or whether the distribution is just due to chance. For this we need to select a statistical test.

Selection of statistical tests

With the data in one hand and our hypotheses in the other, we now need to choose carefully the appropriate statistical test from the wide range of tests available. This is particularly important as choosing an inappropriate test may lead to misleading results which could negate all the effort of collecting the data. Students should beware of selecting over-sophisticated, 'fashionable' tests. We have often found that simple tests, like the one shown later, are perfectly adequate for much of the data that is normally handled in student projects. However, in writing up the tests, it is important to justify why particular tests were used for the data.

Probably the most important factor in selecting a statistical test is the type of measurement scale used (i.e. the type of data). In statistical terms, these measurement scales can be classified as:

Nominal (or categorical) where numbers are used as labels just to classify objects or characteristics and there is no ranking or ordering of categories along any scale. Thus the categories could be presented in any order without changing their meaning. Examples include the numerical coding of country of origin or computer manufacturer.

Ordinal (or ranking) where there is a natural ordering to the categories but we cannot meaningfully measure the distance between 'objects'. Examples include 'very satisfied', 'satisfied', 'dissatisfied' and 'very dissatisfied', as well as most responses on Likert scales.

Interval (or cardinal) is the same as ordinal, except that distances between any two readings on the scale have some meaning; that is, there is a common unit of measurement and the ratio of any two measurement intervals does not depend on the unit of measurement. An example here would be temperature, which can be measured in Fahrenheit or Celsius. *Ratio* is the same as interval, except that the scale has a true zero point, for example length or weight.

Where there is mixed data, for example, nominal and ordinal, it is recommended to take a conservative approach and, in selecting a statistical test or measure of association, to treat all the data as nominal (the 'lower' category).

Worked example

Our data in the ERP support centre example is a mixture of nominal (location of ERP support centre) and ordinal (degree of satisfaction) and we wish to perform a test to see whether there is any association between the location of the support centre and the degree of satisfaction. One of the easiest tests of association to perform, and one that is also highly tolerant in terms of the type of data, is the chi-square test.

Having selected the appropriate test, one then has to carry it out, normally using the available statistical software. Again, this is not trivial and readers should ensure that they understand what they are testing as well as the mass of figures presented by the software. It is a sound principle to write down the hypothesis that one is testing (as well as the null hypothesis).

The chi-square test involves calculating the expected values for each cell, based on the row and column totals, and comparing them with the actual (observed) values. The expected values imply no relationship between the variables, which if they match the data would cause us to reject H_1 the hypothesis that a relationship exists. The calculation comprises summing the relative differences for each cell in the table, but this is performed automatically by the software.

However, in our example, as is often the case in practice, we cannot apply chi-square immediately because of one of its inherent restrictions that the expected value for each cell should exceed 5. Often the data collected is too finely grained to provide any evidence of association; that is, there are too many categories for each question and the number of responses in each category is relatively low. This can be overcome to some extent by 'collapsing' the categories. In other words, adjacent categories can be combined together to give an increased number of responses in each category. Care has to be taken, however, that such combinations are meaningful. In our case, it makes sense to collapse the rows, as in Table 8.2.

Table 8.2 Example of a cross-tabulation with collapsed categories

	ERP support centre		
	Local	HQ	Total
Satisfied	16	8	24
Dissatisfied	5	9	14
Total	21	17	38

The calculation gives a value for the chi-square statistic of 23.64 which, when checked against statistical tables, shows that the probability of H_1 (a relationship exists) is very high; in fact, the probability that the results are due to chance is less than 0.001.

Often, rather than just showing that a relationship (association) exists, we wish to measure the strength of that relationship, which means using a measure of association. There are various such measures available and students should refer to Healey (2002) for help in selecting the test that suits the nature of their data. In our example, *phi* (φ) is an appropriate measure and this calculation results in a value for *phi* (φ) of 0.79, which is fairly strong. The *phi* measure is used for nominal data in 2×2 tables. Where there are more than two categories for a variable, Cramer's V is recommended for nominal data. Most measures of association have a range from 0 to 1, where 0 means no relationship and 1 implies perfect correlation.

Strictly speaking, *phi* and Cramer's V are indices of the strength of the association and not direct measures. Over the last few years, proportional reduction in error (PRE) measures of association have become more popular because they are more stable and more meaningful. The recommended PRE measure of association for nominal data is *lambda* (λ). For a detailed comparison, students are referred to Healey (2002, ch. 13).

Aspects of statistical tests of association

Students should appreciate the distinction between the strength of a relationship and its statistical significance. One can have a very weak relationship with a high level of statistical significance (i.e. it is highly likely that it exists) and vice versa. Regardless of the statistic used, there are normally three aspects of a relationship that should be considered:

Statistical significance refers to whether we have enough evidence to assume that the relationship is more than just due to chance. This is normally shown as the probability that the relationship is due to chance. For example, a significance of 0.05 means that there is a 1 in 20 chance that the results are due to chance and 0.001 that the probability is 1 in 1000.

Strength refers to the degree of the relationship; that is, whether there are large differences between categories. The correlation statistics normally vary between 0 (no relationship) and 1 (complete dependence) but a value of, say, 0.70 would suggest a fairly strong relationship.

Direction, which is normally indicated by the sign (plus or minus) of the statistic, refers to whether the relationship is positive or negative. Strictly speaking, this is only meaningful for ordinal or interval data but, for example with our case, the direction is obvious from the data.

Ordinal measurement scales

Ordinal scales tend to be of two types. Either they have many different possible values and resemble interval variables, in which case they are known as continuous ordinal variables, or they have relatively few possible values (no more than five or six) and these are known as collapsed ordinal variables. An example of the former could be the case where we are studying the expertise of individuals in a company on the basis of their (hierarchical) staff grade and there are, say, ten grades. An example of the latter would be a 5-point attitude scale between very satisfied and very dissatisfied.

These two types of scale call forth two slightly different measures of association. For the continuous ordinal variables, Spearman's *rho* (r_s) is recommended while gamma (*G*) is normally used for collapsed ordinal variables. Gamma is a PRE-based statistic while *rho* is not, but a PRE interpretation is possible by

---

BOX 8.3

Golden rules of inference

- Clarify the hypotheses
- Only test for meaningful relationships
- Eyeballing can be as effective as statistical computation
- Know thy data – nominal, ordinal or interval
- Distinguish between significance and strength
- Keep a weather eye on the data
- Do not become infatuated with the sophistication of the analysis

squaring *rho* (r_s^2). These statistics indicate the power of any relationship and both can be tested for statistical significance using a Z distribution.

An example of the use of gamma could be a comparison between the length of service of information systems managers (classified as low, medium and high) and their recorded stress levels (again classified as low, medium and high).

When making inferences, the golden rules in Box 8.3 must be kept in mind. It often happens that responses to questionnaires are similar and seem to form some sort of pattern such that there is a relationship between the answers to particular questions. Sometimes this may be a result of certain latent (also known as hidden or intervening) variables that are operating outside the question responses. These variables may turn out to be ones that might be useful in summarizing the responses and can be teased out by the use of factor analysis supported by appropriate software. This technique examines the correlation between responses to questions by the different respondents. Its application can be seen in a study by Boynton *et al.* (1994) where 42 items (question responses) concerning information technology management process effectiveness are factored into 8 factors (including project management, strategic management and resource planning) and 23 items concerning the information technology management climate are factored into 6 factors (e.g. planning commitment, information sharing).

Interval measurement scales

Where we have interval (or ratio) data to analyse, we can then use parametric statistics, which are more familiar to most undergraduates. In fact, in many cases, if we have a large number (more than 100) of observations on an ordinal scale, parametric statistics are valid.

A typical measure of association is Pearson's *r* (or r^2 in PRE terms) and significance can be tested using the *t*-test, which is used for comparing two independent samples, and analysis of variance (with its associated *F*-test) for comparing a number of related samples. Thus, for example, a *t*-test might be appropriate for comparing the responses of managers with those of clerks, while analysis of variance would be more appropriate for comparing responses between the six operating divisions of a company. More details of parametric statistics can be found in Healey (2002) and the information systems literature is full of examples of their use (e.g. Dennis *et al.*, 1999; Fichman, 2001).

Statistical analysis is not easy but it can be useful, provided that the student keeps a weather eye on the data and does not become infatuated with the analysis.

Golden rules of statistical interpretation

- Correlation does not imply causation
- Relationships (or apparent relationships) require explanations
- Beware the temptation to generalize – 'one swallow does not make a summer'

Interpreting the results

Finally, having carried out the (mostly statistical) analysis, the student must then interpret the results, whether there is evidence of statistical association or not. Again, care must be taken here and the golden rules given in Box 8.4 would serve as useful pointers.

Where there is some degree of correlation, care must be taken in interpreting the message from the data. Correlation does not imply causation; just because there is a relationship between A and B does not mean that A causes B or vice versa. Often there is a hidden intervening variable. De Vaus (1986) provides a good example of a spurious relationship which 'shows' that the strength of peace movements is correlated with the outbreak of war. Direct causation is out of the question, peace movements do not cause war. Instead, there is an intervening variable, the level of international tension, which is likely to increase both the strength of peace movements and the potential for the outbreak of war. Similarly, just because there is no statistical evidence of association does not mean that no relationship exists. It may just mean that we do not have sufficient responses to warrant a statistical result.

Having discovered a meaningful relationship between sets of data, the substantive explanation for the relationship needs to be discussed with relation to the hypotheses formulated and the underlying theoretical framework for the area. It is pointless identifying a relationship without attempting to provide an explanation as to why or how it occurs.

Care should be taken in generalizing any results. Normally we do not have enough data to generalize very far. We have typically only polled a small proportion of the entire population and, of that small sample, perhaps only 20 per cent responded to the survey. Furthermore, there is no reason to believe that the respondents are necessarily representative of the sample, let alone the population. Often respondents are those who feel strongly (either positively or negatively) about an issue and thus there is a built-in bias to most of the surveys that we carry out. This need not detract too much from the results but we must be careful not to make excessive claims based on relatively little data.

We have presented the main stages of analysis (data preparation, description, inference drawing and interpretation) in their ideal sequence. However, students should be aware that, in practice, research projects are less sequential. We all, consciously or unconsciously, start interpreting during the preparation stage and, as suggested above, one often has to return and repeat an earlier stage because of an idea that has arisen during the later stages of the analysis. This is normal practice and such creativity is preferable to a mechanistic approach to research.

This mixing-up of the stages can also apply to the organization of the final report. In writing up this type of data, one needs to choose a structure that is interesting, logical and avoids repetition. In most cases, separating the write-up into description, analysis and interpretation is boring and invites repetition. Based on our experience, it is better to intersperse these elements as much as possible so long as the structure remains logical. For example, it may be appropriate to present the analysis and interpretation of particular data (say, the benefits of ERP systems) immediately after its description, unless the analysis requires the description of other data (perhaps the availability of ERP support centres) that has not yet been described. Furthermore, it is often better to keep the more detailed discussion of the implications to a later 'discussion' chapter. Thus, the final structure of the report needs to be designed carefully to tell an interesting story that flows logically.

Case studies and qualitative analysis

Although survey research is common in information systems research projects, and descriptive and inferential statistics are widely used to describe and derive meaning from quantitative data, there are many occasions when this approach is inappropriate. Individual case studies are typically more manageable for student projects at both undergraduate and Masters levels. For doctoral students, a quantitative approach alone, based on structured questionnaires, can be too insensitive to capture complex and subtle social and behavioural data. In these situations, detailed case studies of a relatively small number of situations are a realistic alternative. Students can then spend long periods of time carrying out (often numerous) in-depth interviews and/or lengthy observations. Such studies normally yield just as much, if not more, data than a survey but this data is predominantly qualitative data: narrative, impressionistic, opinionative or textual, which is not amenable to statistical analysis. However, this does not mean that it cannot be analysed at all; rather, it requires different techniques of analysis, known as qualitative data analysis. This section discusses the inherent characteristics of such analysis and briefly reviews some of the more important techniques.

Over recent years, qualitative analysis has become an area of increasing interest to researchers in many social sciences, including psychology, anthropology, organizational behaviour and social policy. In terms of research traditions, the techniques discussed below are rooted in interpretivism (see Chapter 3), social anthropology and collaborative social research (or action research). Students who wish to study these techniques in more depth are recommended to consult one of the textbooks recommended in the further reading section at the end of this chapter. Their application in information systems research is discussed by Galliers (1992) and Lee (1989) and has figured prominently in conferences on information systems research methods (Mumford *et al.*, 1985; Nissen *et al.*, 1991) and information systems and organizational discourse (Wynn *et al.*, 2002).

Qualitative data: benefits and drawbacks

Qualitative analysis has much to commend it as the close involvement of the researcher in the situation under study facilitates the achievement of considerable insight into the events, actions and actors concerned. The extended face-to-face nature of the research should help to lower the barriers between the researcher and the actors. Explanations for their behaviour and other notions of causality are likely to be suggested by the actors themselves, although of course these may be more espoused than 'actual'. Nevertheless, such methods normally give the researcher considerable flexibility in terms of being able to repeat interviews and observations or change approach, taking different observations and asking different questions of the various actors.

However, qualitative data has certain, rather problematic, characteristics, which set it apart from quantitative data (Miles and Huberman, 1994). It is usually predominantly textual, with a richness that can easily be lost when we attempt to aggregate or summarize it. It can be fairly unstructured and unbounded as it often concerns people's behaviour and trying to understand their perceptions of a particular situation. It is often longitudinal, to a greater or lesser extent, in that observations may continue for an extended period of time and interviews may be repeated at intervals of a few days, weeks or months. The researchers themselves are trying to achieve a holistic, over-arching view, rather than a reductionist selection of particular actions. The end result is typically a curious concoction of description and analysis of a complex mixture of events and actions and the perceptions and value systems of the actors.

In more 'scientific' terms, there are potentially severe drawbacks compared to the classical scientific tradition. First, because it is specific to, at best, a small number of cases (perhaps only one case), it is very hard to generalize to a wider range of situations. Second, the richness and complexity means that the data is often open to a number of very different interpretations, such that researcher bias is a constant danger. Third, researchers involved in dynamic cases where the situation is changing frequently, face inherent problems in trying to make controlled observations (to set against 'control groups'), controlled deductions (using mathematical and statistical methods) and predictions. These aspects make validity and verifiability constant worries for researchers.

These problems are further exacerbated by two important factors: the commonly used inductive approach to theory and the lack of accepted methods and techniques. Often, but not always, rather than taking a deductive approach, where hypotheses are first 'deduced' from existing theory and then tested, researchers adopt more of a grounded theory type of approach to case studies (Glaser and Strauss, 1967). In the latter approach, hypotheses, propositions, themes and classifications are developed (induced) from the data as the study progresses. The notion of dealing with large amounts of 'messy' unstructured data without a set of comforting pre-specified hypotheses could be regarded as either a significant opportunity for original thought or as a recipe for disaster. However, it should be noted that, just because stringent hypotheses have not been developed in advance, does not mean that students are encouraged to drift into the research in an empty-headed fashion. Before applying this approach researchers need to have a good grasp of the theories underlying their research and a well-developed conceptual model of the situation they study. This model may change as the research proceeds but there must always be a firm starting point.

The other significant factor, the lack of accepted methods and techniques, is less of a problem and students should not regard qualitative analysis as a 'black art'. There are numerous robust methods and techniques available, of varying levels of sophistication. We discuss some of the more popular ones later. However, bearing in mind the richness (or messiness) of the data, it is important that students strike a careful balance between an excessively systematic approach and a reliance on research by 'flashes of insight' or 'osmosis'. Each of these elements is necessary but the adoption of either extreme will certainly result in a loss of much of the understanding potentially available.

While the underlying logic is very similar to quantitative analysis, the nature of the data and the associated processes mean that the stages of analysis do not exactly map onto those we used for quantitative analysis. The element of induction means that the boundaries between stages and activities are necessarily even more indistinct. Thus, for example, interpretation naturally intrudes into data preparation as alternative conceptual models are applied in the coding of messy real life data. There is normally a strong element of iteration as fresh ideas emerge and students should repeatedly examine the original data, often gathering additional data to try to confirm any new insights.

Data preparation

The initial problem faced by students applying qualitative approaches to their research is what to do with the huge amounts of data, made up of reams of interview notes, transcripts or observational data, previous reports and historical data, examples of forms and documents used and perhaps audio or video tapes pertaining to the area of study. The solutions available are basic, 'commonsense' ones. First, whether there are a number of separate cases or just one case; there is usually at least one obvious initial way of organizing the data, for example, by company, organizational department or individual interviewee. This may be a fairly rough classification and unsuitable for the final presentation, but it is a starting point. Based on this initial structure, it is possible to gather all the relevant material together, to ensure that nothing is forgotten or mislaid. At this stage, it is often useful to produce a summary sheet for each major data grouping. This should show the 'catalogue' of data; for example, the names of those interviewed, the dates of the interviews and whether recordings were made. It should also contain a very brief overview of the content of the data. This simple technique can be invaluable for keeping track of large amounts of data.

There are a few other pre-analysis techniques that can be useful when dealing with large amounts of textual data. Researchers may write short 'memos' (to themselves) that record certain key thoughts and ideas as they occur. These may concern a particular (often sudden) insight into the situation or perhaps changes that need to be made to the underlying conceptual framework. Similarly, brief anecdotes (or 'vignettes') of specific events or actions may be written up and highlighted where these are particularly insightful or relevant. Finally, especially in a complex, changing situation, researchers may need to pay careful attention to the sequence of events and actions, ensuring that this has been recorded accurately before any attempt at interpretation is made. The results of these simple activities should be kept in the project diary to ensure that they are not lost in the mass of raw data.

Coding

Somehow, the large amounts of textual data collected have to be presented, ultimately to the readers of the final report, but first to the researcher. This needs to be done in a readable fashion that provides a firm foundation for interpretation. In addition, this process of summarization and refinement should not lose too much of the richness of the original data. Simple graphical techniques are available that, when used sensitively, can summarize many pages of text and bring out the essence of the description. These are mostly based on tables (or matrices) or some form of network representation. Tables are particularly helpful to highlight key features of one or more cases (with different cases forming the columns of the table) according to the key criteria or structures of the current conceptual framework. Network representations, such as context charts and cognitive maps, depict aspects of the situation in terms of nodes and arcs. Such networks are particularly useful for showing sequential relationships or relationships between concepts or roles. Some networks are appropriate for comparing multiple cases; for example, decision trees show individual cases as the 'leaves' of the tree.

Following the schema of Flick (2002) we will discuss coding and categorizing of data in this section and then turn to the more 'sequential analyses' in the next section. Unlike the coding of quantitative data, the coding of qualitative data necessitates a fair amount of interpretation. The coding activity is a way of assigning meaning to the data, according to the researcher's conceptual model at the time. In our experience, in information systems this usually involves summarizing and reducing the complexity of real life. However, in qualitative analysis it is more likely that the researcher's conceptual model will change as the research proceeds, in which case recoding may be required.

Our first technique, theoretical coding (see Strauss and Corbin, 1990), is associated with developing grounded theory (Glaser and Strauss, 1967) and assumes that there is no a priori theory. Thus, it is very open and suitable for virtually any problem domain. Starting from the combined texts (e.g. all the interview transcripts), concepts are identified and then categorized into more generic concepts and relationships are identified between concepts. Thus networks of concepts and their relationships can be developed from these concepts that spring from the text. The steps of theoretical coding are as follows:

- *Open coding* – the original text is segmented and concepts (or codes) within it are identified by examining the text in detail. Initial categories (groups of concepts) are formed.
- *Axial coding* – the categories, concepts and relationships are then refined.
- *Selective coding* – refinement is continued at a higher level of abstraction in order to tease out the core category and the central storyline.

The second technique, thematic coding (Flick, 1995), assumes that the initial grouping of interviewees and the questions asked relates to a formulated research question or theory. This technique matches, for example, the use of semi-structured interviews. Open and selective coding are carried out for each interviewee so that themes and categories are developed on a case by case basis. These themes and categories can then be compared across cases (interviewees) as well as against the research question and theoretical framework.

A third technique, content analysis, involves the application of an existing categorization scheme to the text, rather than developing one based on the data as in the above two techniques. It is a rigid and systematic, classical approach aimed at reducing the amount of material to be interpreted. Thus the research question and analytical techniques should be carefully fixed in advance. There is typically a quantitative (counting) element, as the frequency of keywords (terms) is produced, as well as more qualitative interpretation of the text. Further details can be found in Bauer (2000).

The above techniques are, to a greater or lesser extent, systematic and transparent. They can be used in a variety of situations and can normally deal with large quantities of text. However, too much reliance on frequency distributions of words may produce distortions depending upon the interviewees' style of talking and how they utilize their vocabularies. Also, the absence of particular terms or concepts may turn out to be just as important as their presence or frequency. Nevertheless these techniques suit situations where the researcher is trying to find out how the interviewees conceptualize topics; for example, their view of a new technology, such as ERP systems or e-commerce, or a new way of working, such as virtual teams.

Sequential analyses

While the coding techniques above are useful for analysing 'static' topics, in many cases the researcher is more interested in a sequence of events or how the interviewee perceives a 'story'. In information systems, two techniques are often employed: discourse analysis and narrative analysis.

Discourse analysis (Gill, 2000) can be distinguished from conversation analysis by its focus on the content of the discourse, rather than its linguistic conventions. It can be applied to conversations, interviews and reports. It fits with notions of social construction where the researcher is exploring representations of the social reality of interviewees. According to Gill, there are four main themes:

- A concern with a 'text' in its own right, rather than as an instrument to get behind the representation to the reality itself.
- Language is constructive – interviewees use language to construct their text.
- A text (or discourse) is a form of social action taking place in a particular context.
- A text is organized rhetorically – for example, in order to persuade the reader or listener of the rightness of a particular point of view.

A good example of the use of discourse analysis in the information systems literature is Thompson's (2002) paper on information technology in developing countries.

Narrative analysis (Bruner, 1987) is useful when the researcher is enquiring into a sequence of events, for example, a failed information systems implementation. Narrative is a powerful means of 'telling a story' including both the sequence of events and the meaning that links the events. The researcher normally interviews the various stakeholders (IT Department, users, vendors etc.) to obtain *their* versions of the story. These are likely to be different as one party may blame the others and these narratives are evidently socially constructed. Thus, there is probably no 'true' representation of events but rather various constructions. Nevertheless, the differences between the various constructions can be informative. There are various versions of narrative analysis in the social science literature but the usual first step is to take the text and strip out all the non-narrative material before analysing what remains. Some researchers are more concerned with the process of narrative construction, rather than the narrative itself.

Interpretation

In the area of interpretation, the drawing up of conclusions and verifying those conclusions, qualitative analysis is often viewed as being particularly problematic as it normally lacks the comforting support of inferential statistics. One danger in such research is to focus solely on the description of what happened in the situation in question. While such narrative story-telling can be interesting and entertaining, it is very easy for inexperienced researchers to omit elements of analysis altogether and produce a 'flat', anecdotal report. Remember: all the best stories have messages and morals and so analysis, in the form of interpretation, is essential. Moreover, the adoption of certain, 'commonsense' techniques can both reduce the researcher's uncertainty as to how to go about interpretation, as well as forcing some element of interpretation on to the data. Lee (1994) provides a useful discussion of the nature of interpretation in a case study on electronic mail.

Miles and Huberman (1994, ch. 10) propose 13 such commonsense 'tactics' to assist interpretation. Their first group of tactics is based on a careful study of the data collected. These include techniques such as content analysis (discussed earlier) where researchers examine the data closely in order to identify meaningful patterns or themes. However, while doing this it is a good idea to 'think through' explicitly the plausibility of the proposed explanation: Is it reasonable? Does it really fit the data? Another technique is to try to cluster cases together based on perceived similarities and differences; for example, all the accountants interviewed may have responded in the same fashion. In some instances, it can be insightful to construct metaphors (Morgan, 1980), which can add further richness and vividness to data, although there are obvious dangers of utilizing inappropriate metaphors that conceal more than they reveal.

Although data in such studies are fundamentally qualitative, the opportunities to 'count' things, as in content analysis, can be extended to, for example, counting the number of complaints per month received by a help desk. Thus, the quantitative data can be used to throw further light on the situation. Explicit comparisons between cases, or between interviewees, are an obvious technique to examine similarities and differences (see Eisenhardt, 1989). In addition, where a particular area, or aspect of the study, starts to become important, it can be a good idea to partition variables that have become too monolithic and insensitive into more specific variables.

Miles and Huberman's (1994) second group of tactics takes the opposite approach and involves 'getting outside' the case and taking a more abstract view of the data. Thus, it may be appropriate to try to subsume details of the particular into the general, in order to remove extraneous detail. A related technique is factoring, where individual variables are grouped into composite, second-order 'factors' which again should remove excessive complexity but without affecting the overall analysis. In the same spirit, in examining relations between concepts, intervening (but unstated) concepts can be insightful.

The final aim is to systematically construct a coherent understanding of the situation and the data collected. This typically involves building a logical chain of evidence and confirming that the final conceptual model is theoretically coherent. See Box 8.5 for the golden rules of qualitative analysis.

BOX 8.5

Golden rules of qualitative analysis

- Build a conceptual model early on but be prepared to refine it during the analysis
- Aim for analysis rather than anecdote
- Try to summarize without losing the richness of the context
- Build up and communicate an understanding of the case(s)
- Worry about validity and verifiability

Testing

The nature of qualitative data and the inherently subjective way in which it has been collected, prepared, presented and interpreted means that more attention needs to be paid to testing the interpretations finally arrived at. Again, Miles and Huberman (1994) provide a useful set of tactics for testing the findings. At first glance, these may seem fairly obvious but it is all too easy to neglect this important aspect, especially when the researcher is closely involved in the case and has become convinced of the validity of his/her interpretation.

There is normally a need to check the quality of the data. Is it really representative of the study situation? Have important aspects been concealed or inaccurately perceived due to the bias of the researcher? The notion of triangulation, using other sources of data to counteract any bias in the data collection methods, is useful here. For example, there may be the possibility of using independent measures of the same variable. Similarly using interpretations of the same data by other people can counter researcher bias. A consideration of data quality often reveals variances in reliability, perhaps because of the way particular interviews were conducted. In this case, the more reliable data can be given greater weight in the analysis.

One approach, that may appear rather painful at first, is to search for evidence that somehow disproves or casts doubts on the findings. This may involve a detailed examination of 'outliers' (variables/cases whose values do not fit the findings very well) or extreme cases, for example, very large or very small companies. Similarly, any 'surprising' data should be followed up and explained.

The final explanations or interpretations arrived at should be tested, perhaps by carrying out if-then tests, either on paper or empirically. Students should always be on the lookout for spurious relations, which are as common with qualitative data as with quantitative data. Ideally, given the time and opportunity, it would be preferable to replicate the findings in other situations but often this is infeasible. Alternative explanations should be considered explicitly and evidence presented for their rejection. Finally, it is an excellent technique to ask the actors within the situation what they think of the findings and interpretation. Obtaining feedback from the informants can be extremely useful and, depending upon the situation, it is a polite way of ending a researcher's involvement.

Presentation

In presenting narratives, it is often useful to impose a simple structure on the complexity of life. One such structure separates out the main episode (comprising a number of events), which has a particular start and a particular ending, from:

- Prior events
- Later events
- Contemporaneous events (that somehow affect the main episode)
- Related events (that are somehow affected by the main episode).

Clearly one has to take care not to lose the richness of the 'story' through the imposition of this, or any other, structure.

As with survey research, the judicious use of verbatim quotes from people often adds an authenticity of tone and colour to the narrative. People often have powers of expression based upon many years' involvement with the situation, and that cannot be achieved by even the most sensitive researcher.

For presentation in the final report, a question that frequently arises for studies made up of a small number of cases is whether to write each one up individually and then compare the cases or whether to present the entire findings as a comparison. The first approach allows each case to be considered as a whole, including all the various aspects and complexities, so that an interim conclusion can easily be drawn for each case. On the other hand, the second approach emphasizes comparison as all the cases can be discussed, criterion by criterion. Much depends upon the nature of the study but, for relatively simple cases at least, the latter approach is probably preferable. This approach avoids too much repetition of data in the findings and discussion chapters of the report, or requiring the reader to remember data over various chapters. However, with such a report structure, it is essential that the background or context of each case is discussed in an early chapter to give the reader a basis for comparison. Another option is to provide a case-by-case structure as an appendix.

For good examples of the use of narrative in the information systems literature, readers are referred to Kumar *et al.* (1998) who tell the story of the failure of SPRINTEL, a videotex system in Italy, and McGrath's (2002) account of the long-running problems in implementing a command and control system in the London Ambulance Service.

Software for qualitative analysis

Students wishing to code and analyse large blocks of textual data may find the increasing range of qualitative analysis software helpful. However, students should appreciate from the start that the 'power' of this type of software to 'do' analysis is nowhere near comparable to the equivalent statistical analysis packages operating on quantitative data. Packages such as Nud*ist and Atlas/ti can be classified as 'code-based theory building' software (Flick, 2002) based on their capability for manipulating concepts but students are warned that they must provide all the conceptual understanding themselves. In our opinion, such software should be viewed more as sophisticated data administration tools and they are certainly no substitute for the immersion of the student in the data and the resulting personal interpretation of the data by the student. They can take over much of the low-level, 'no-brain', text processing but even the gains from this need to be set against the time needed to learn how to use the software. They are certainly worthwhile for large-scale or frequent text analysis but their value for smaller one-off projects is questionable.

The facilities provided by such software usually include:

- Construction of a textual database
- Search and retrieval facilities that are more refined than the average word-processing package
- Support for coding
- Counting capability regarding index terms (defined concepts)
- The linking of index terms
- The insertion of codes or comments into a text
- Production of network graphs of index terms.

Students who are interested in exploring this software further are referred to Flick (2002, ch. 20) and Kelle (2000). Many universities run short courses on this type of software and the online tutorials included with the software are also quite effective.

Combining quantitative and qualitative analysis

The two major approaches to analysis described in this chapter are certainly not mutually exclusive. Rather, they should be seen as complementary toolkits, each containing a set of tools, any of which may be relevant to a particular problem situation. In our view, only purists discount either toolkit at the expense of the other. Much information systems research has both quantitative and qualitative elements and considerable additional insight can normally be gained by combining the approaches.

However, students should be aware that the approaches require different skills: the mathematics of quantitative analysis and the rather broader understanding of qualitative research. Nevertheless, there is a very important skills set common to both approaches and that is the ability to design a research study and apply analysis techniques that accurately and comprehensively meet the objectives of the study. Conceptual frameworks, the identification and coding of variables, and the need to avoid spurious relationships are common to each approach. This is also true of the need to manage the analysis task, to prevent the gaps associated with too little analysis or the confusion and delay which normally stems from too much analysis.

Summary

- Appreciate the cycle of data analysis and devote appropriate time to each activity – preparing the data, presenting the data, drawing inferences and interpreting results.
- Analysis is important; it distinguishes a good academic piece of work from mere journalism. It should be done conscientiously and students should be aware of the potential benefits and difficulties of adopting alternative approaches.
- Analysis is not easy. It requires thought and practice and should be seen as an exercise in understanding rather than the mere manipulation of ill-understood techniques.

Further reading

For statistical techniques the text by Healey (2002) cited earlier is recommended while for qualitative analysis, the following texts, also cited in the References, provide useful guidance: Bauer and Gaskell (2000), Denzin and Lincoln (2000), Flick (2002), Miles and Huberman (1994).

References

Baroudi, J. J. and W. J. Orlikowski (1989) 'The problem of statistical power in MIS research'. *MIS Quarterly*, vol.13, no.1, pp. 87–106.

Bauer, M. W. (2000) 'Classical content analysis: A review', in M. W. Bauer and G. Gaskell (eds), *Qualitative Researching with Text, Image and Sound* (London: Sage), pp. 131–51.

Bauer, M. W. and G. Gaskell (eds) (2000) *Qualitative Researching with Text, Image and Sound* (London: Sage).

Boynton, A. C., R. W. Zmud, and G. C. Jacobs (1994) 'The influence of IT management practice on IT use in large organizations', *MIS Quarterly*, vol.18, no.3, pp. 299–318.

Bruner, J. (1987) 'Life as narrative', *Social Research*, vol.54, pp. 11–32.

De Vaus, D. A. (1986) *Surveys in Social Research* (London: George Allen and Unwin).

Dennis, A. R., J. E. Aronson, W. G. Heninger, and E. D. Walker (1999) 'Structuring time and task in electronic brainstorming', *MIS Quarterly*, vol.23, no.1, pp. 95–108.

Denzin, N. and Y. S. Lincoln (eds) (2000) *Handbook of Qualitative Research*, second edn (London: Sage).

Eisenhardt, K. M. (1989) 'Building theories from case study research', *Academy of Management Review*, vol.14, no.4, pp. 532–50.

Fichman, R. G. (2001) 'The role of aggregation in the measurement of IT-related organizational innovation'. *MIS Quarterly*, vol.25, no.4, pp. 427–55.

Flick, U. (1995) 'Social representations', in R. Harré, J. Smith and L. V. Langenhove (eds) *Rethinking Psychology* (London: Sage), pp. 70–96.

Flick, U. (2002) *An Introduction to Qualitative Research*, second edn (London: Sage).

Galliers, R. D. (1992) *Information Systems Research: Issues Methods and Practical Guidelines* (Oxford: Blackwells).

Gill, R. (2000) 'Discourse analysis', in M. W. Bauer and G. Gaskell (eds), *Qualitative Researching with Text, Image and Sound* (London: Sage), pp. 172–90.

Glaser, B. G. and A. L. Strauss (1967) *The Discovery of Grounded Theory: Strategies for Qualitative Research* (Chicago, IL: Aldine).

Healey, J. F. (2002) *Statistics: A Tool for Social Research*, sixth edn (London: Wadsworth).

Kelle, U. (2000) 'Computer-assisted analysis: Coding and indexing', in M .W. Bauer and G. Gaskell (eds), *Qualitative Researching with Text, Image and Sound* (London: Sage), pp. 282–98.

Kumar, K., H. G. Van Dissel, and P. Bielle, (1998) 'The Merchant of Prato revisited: Towards a third rationality of information systems', *MIS Quarterly*, June, pp. 199–226.

Lee, A. S. (1989) 'A scientific methodology for MIS case studies', *MIS Quarterly*, vol.13, no.1, pp. 33–50.

Lee, A. S. (1994) 'Electronic mail as a medium for rich communication: An empirical investigation using hermeneutic interpretation', *MIS Quarterly*, vol.18, no.2, pp. 143–57.

McGrath, K. (2002) 'In a mood to make sense of technology: A longitudinal study of discursive practices at the London Ambulance Service', in E. H. Wynn, E. A. Whitley, M. D. Myers and J. I. DeGross (eds) (2002) *Global and Organizational Discourse about Information Technology* (Boston, MA: Kluwer), pp. 485–506.

Miles, M. B. and A. M. Huberman (1994) *Qualitative Data Analysis*, second edn (Thousand Oaks, CA: Sage).

Morgan, G. (1980) 'Paradigms, metaphors, and puzzle-solving in organizational theory', *Administrative Science Quarterly*, vol.25, no.4, pp. 605–22

Mumford, E., R. Hirschheim, G. Fitzgerald and A. T. Wood-Harper (eds) (1985) *Research Methods in Information Systems* (Amsterdam: North Holland).

Nissen, H-E., H. K. Klein, and R. Hirschheim (eds) (1991) *Information Systems Research: Contemporary Approaches and Emergent Traditions* (Amsterdam: North Holland).

Strauss, A. L. and J. Corbin (1990) *Basics of Qualitative Research* (London: Sage).

Thompson, M. (2002) 'ICT, power, and developmental discourse: A critical analysis', in E. H. Wynn, E. A. Whitley, M. D. Myers and J. I. DeGross (eds) (2002) *Global and Organizational Discourse about Information Technology* (Boston: Kluwer), pp. 348–73.

Wynn, E. H., E. A. Whitley, M. D. Myers, and J.I. DeGross (eds) (2002) *Global and Organizational Discourse about Information Technology* (Boston: Kluwer).

Writing a project report

- ■ **If English is not your native language**
- ■ **A writer's tools**
- ■ **General hints on writing**
- ■ **Writing style**
- ■ **Writer's block**
- ■ **Charts, diagrams and tables**
- ■ **Structure of a project report**
- ■ **The body of the report**
- ■ **Questions of layout**
- ■ **Making a presentation**

For many students the project report will be the longest single piece of writing that they have ever attempted. For some, the idea of writing 8000+ words may seem a very daunting prospect, more daunting perhaps than actually undertaking the study itself. For people who are worried about this, there are two forms of reassurance that we can give.

The first is to say that if you throw yourself into your research with enthusiasm and commitment, then the words will follow. When you have something to say, you will find a way to say it. Also, if you approach the project systematically and in manageable steps, then the individual items or sections that you produce along the way will each themselves be relatively small and manageable. You should also make sure that you write regularly and often, so that writing becomes a commonplace activity, and not something special.

The second way to gain assurance in tackling writing tasks is to become interested in the art of writing itself. If you can see writing, using language to communicate, as a challenging and satisfying activity, and one that can engage your intellect, then you will be a long way towards breaking down any barriers. However good or bad you feel you are as a writer, it is never too late to improve your ability. If you do adopt such a positive approach then you should look around to seek out any help that is provided within your college, or through using books. It is also important to share your writings with other people and to seek their feedback and advice in order to improve.

It may seem rather strange or inappropriate to take a particular interest in how to set about the task of writing at the *end* of many years of education. Writing is, after all, a subject that disappears from the school curriculum around the age of 14 and by the time students have passed through university they have probably written many hundreds of essays and taken numerous exams. Even so, it is important to remember that you are probably going to do a lot more writing in the years ahead, and that you are often going to be judged by the quality of that work. Any investment that you make now in improving your ability to write will be repaid many times over.

If English is not your native language

For those students for whom English is not their native language these encouragements are even more significant. In Britain, as in many other countries, a substantial proportion of students in higher education come from abroad and may be studying for the first time in English. If you are one of these, you need to take particular care to work at your language skills, both as a reader, as a writer and as a presenter, and to make use of any special help that is available to you, for example in a university language centre.

You gained entry to university on the basis of your prior study, and you certainly should be capable, in the general sense, of performing well and gaining benefit from your courses. However, if your language skills are weak and if you do not make specific efforts to improve them, then you may not benefit as much as you could from your period of study. Perhaps the best advice to give is to live your student life 'in English'. Make English speaking friends, participate in events and activities that develop your language skills, and practice your English at every opportunity. Unfortunately, it is quite common for students from the same country to stick together, live together, eat lunch together and study together. Such students, as a result, do not develop their English skills, and this can seriously handicap them when it comes to project work. If you tend to behave in this way then you need to make some real efforts to break out of the small circle of your fellow country men and women.

For students from other countries it is often not just a case of developing English language skills, but also of making adjustments to a new and different style of study, and to being assessed according to different criteria. For example, in our experience students are sometimes surprised at the emphasis placed in Britain on students' original work. Indeed, some students come from educational traditions in which they are expected to faithfully learn and repeat material presented by professors. In the British tradition a student is expected to do more; teachers are interested in what you think, how you see the world, and what original contributions you can make. Repeating established ideas without subjecting them to your own critical assessment is not much appreciated.

Such issues of what is expected from students often comes to a head in project work, where it may seem easy and appropriate just to find and repeat standard accounts of a topic. However, you need to understand that examiners are looking for evidence of your own distinctive work and of your ability to be creative and original in your thinking. To make this impression you have to be able to write well and express yourself with confidence. Any confusion as to what is expected can become really serious if it leads students to directly copy from other work. Remember, if you copy work without referencing it then you risk being accused of plagiarism (see Chapter 6). Neither weak skills in the use of English, nor an appeal to some other tradition of higher education, will be seen as a valid excuse.

A writer's tools

A writer needs a place to write, somewhere quiet and relaxing with a minimum of disturbance. A writer also needs to be provided with the appropriate tools, and today these extend beyond paper, pen and dictionary.

The wordprocessor

Any student of information systems will be expected to know about wordprocessors; they may not, however, have had much practice in using them in earnest, and in particular, in using all the features that such systems now offer. A full-scale project is the ideal opportunity to learn, and it is almost always a requirement that reports are prepared in this way. A nicely produced, well laid out report is both attractive to handle and easy to read, as well as demonstrating the writer's ability to produce such documents. Using a computer also demands a basic level of keyboard and typing skill, and it may be an idea to use typing tutorial software to brush-up such abilities.

Wordprocessors are more than smart typewriters. Features such as user-defined styles, outlining, multiple fonts, grammar checkers, indexing, table of contents generation, and the ability to incorporate graphic images provide the opportunity to produce a document of a very high standard with much less effort than in the past. For many people, the most useful feature of a word-processor is the spelling and grammar checker, but this feature should be used critically. Spelling checkers may have inadequate dictionaries and grammar checkers can be just wrong about certain phrases or constructions; do not always take the 'correct' word offered without thinking. Remember too that spell checkers can do nothing about words that are correctly spelled but inappropriately used; for example, 'principle' for 'principal' or 'form' for 'from'.

For most people the real benefit of a wordprocessor is that text can be worked on in a somewhat random fashion, adding a paragraph here and adjusting a sentence there. In this way it is possible to develop a document incrementally and refine the expression of ideas. That said, it is probably best to draft the main sections of a report in one go, getting the main ideas down and working on the sequence in which they are presented. Wordprocessors that support an outlining function make this a very natural procedure, but any system will allow the writer rough-out a report in terms of headings and subheadings, opening sentences or introductory paragraphs.

It is also a good idea to print out periodically a version of work in progress, and to edit it by hand. For most people it is easier to read documents and spot mistakes on paper (rather than on the screen) and also the paper version gives a much better impression of the feel of the whole document.

For some people, the wordprocessor leads to an extreme reluctance to delete anything once it has been typed in, and tired old sentences and paragraphs reappear time after time. If you feel that this is your problem (you probably do not, but somebody may tell you), then *dare to delete*. If the ideas are really important then you will no doubt find another way to express them.

If there are really difficult parts of a project to write, then it may be a good idea to work on them in longhand; that is, after all, the style of writing that we have most practice with. For many (especially less experienced) users of word-processors, the 'pen?paper interface' holds fewer distractions and concerns than a keyboard and screen. Writing in longhand also allows you to work anywhere that suits your mood and may liberate you from a noisy computer room.

Reference databases

All projects require that some references to other literature be given, and some projects require a substantial number. The simplest tool to use for this is a stack of note cards as described in Chapter 6. However, if many references are to be used, a reference database or bibliography maker program can be invaluable. Programs such as *EndNote* and *ProCite* (www.endnote.com, www.procite.com) allow you to enter bibliographic details into a database, and search, sort and print lists of references. These programs also work as add-ins for some wordprocessors, allowing you to write and select references as you go along, and to produce an up-to-date bibliography for any document you write. They also provide a variety of reference formats suitable for different types of document, and may even be able to 'capture' bibliographic details direct from your library's computerized catalogue.

When using computers to store any data or text it is important to back-up work regularly. By the time a few weeks have passed, the materials on the computer, in various files, will be very valuable and it is important to keep multiple generational back-up copies as you go along. Such back-ups should be stored in a safe place, preferably away from your usual place of work. You should also take precautions against computer viruses and follow any advice that is offered by the staff of your university's computer services unit. As a specialist in information systems, nobody will have much sympathy if you lose all your work because of a system crash or a bad disk if you do not have adequate back-ups.

A dictionary and thesaurus

All writers need to use a general dictionary. It is not just a question of how to spell a word, but of what precisely a word means and how it should be used. Certain specialist dictionaries may be useful too, for example the *Penguin Dictionary of Information Technology and Computer Science* or the *Blackwell Encyclopaedic Dictionary of Management Information Systems*. A thesaurus, such as Roget's, can help a writer to find the right word, providing synonyms and antonyms.

Most wordprocessors contain a thesaurus function alongside a spelling checker. For example, in the thesaurus of the wordprocessor this book was written with (Word) the word *technology* generates the following: skill; knowledge; expertise; know how; equipment. Is one of these words more appropriate to your needs? Interestingly, and showing that computers are not infallible, for the word *information* the thesaurus gives the following: in order; in sequence; in turn; in rank; in a row. The computer has misinterpreted the word *information* as being *in formation* – not much help! If you do use a thesaurus, be careful not to overdo it – too many different words for the same thing can be just as distracting (agitating, troubling, disturbing, worrying) as lack of variety (heterogeneity, dissimilarity ...).

Style and writing guides

There are many books that can help students to become better writers and provide guidance as to how to present certain types of information.

References to a number of such texts are given at the end of this chapter in the further reading section. If you have any doubts as to your ability as a writer then these guides may be of great help. Not that they can transform your approach over night, but they can help to heighten awareness and to identify common errors.

General hints on writing

In writing, we are all dependent upon the use of grammar, a system of rules that should determine what is acceptable and what is unacceptable. The unacceptable includes the unintelligible and the misleading, as well as the plain 'bad form'. Really poor writing style may be sufficiently unacceptable for a project to be failed by examiners, regardless of content.

We use language to transfer ideas and if our usage of language is un-acceptable to the reader/listener, this will severely detract from our ability to transfer these ideas successfully. However, languages are living things and, as time goes by, grammatical rules change such that certain sentence constructions and uses of words that are acceptable today would have been frowned upon as little as twenty years ago. Languages are permanently in transition and so, at any one time, there will be various constructions whose legitimacy is uncertain. For example, split infinitives ('to critically evaluate'; 'to boldly go') were seen as definitely 'bad grammar' until very recently, but are now becoming more acceptable. However, good writing is much more than just the use of correct grammar. A project report's grammar may be faultless but its style so appalling that it is confusing, incomprehensible or boring in the extreme. In this book we cannot give a full account of all aspects of good writing, even if we were qualified to do so, but based on our experience of supervising and marking information systems projects, we offer the following simple hints and warn of certain common and annoying errors. Space does not permit the mention of more than a few of the most common grammatical mistakes found in reports. If you feel that you need to brush up on your basic grammar skills, then consult one of the texts described in the further reading section of this chapter.

Basic grammar

English text should be written in sentences, and every sentence should include a main verb. Capital letters are used at the start of sentences and for proper names. They should not be used at random for what you see as key phrases such as 'Information Technology' or 'Expert Systems'.

English text is split up into paragraphs. Each paragraph should convey one main idea. That idea should usually be found in one sentence of the paragraph. This may be the first sentence of a paragraph, or it may be in the middle or at the end. The other sentences in a paragraph should introduce or amplify this main idea. Following on from this observation, a good way to summarize a body of text is to take a single sentence from each paragraph. This should convey the overall meaning of the text. If it does not, then there is a problem. Some people recommend this 'single sentence' technique as a powerful way of working with the overall structure of a text. Some advisers may even ask for a draft of a project report or essay in this form.

Apostrophes are used to denote some form of possession (or relationship), such as 'Tony's terminal' or 'the organizations' managers' (where this refers to more than one organization). A common mistake is to use 'it's' to denote possession. 'It's' is a short form of 'it is' and the correct word in this context is 'its'; for example 'a computer and its peripherals'.

Use a single space between words, and a single or double space between sentences. When using brackets do not leave a space after the opening bracket or before the closing bracket (this does not look very good). Spaces should not precede full stops, commas, colons or semi-colons. If your work does become full of extra spaces, then they can usually be removed by the search and replace function.

Writing style

In terms of style, perhaps the first point is to 'know your reader'. In this case the primary reader comprises the examiners for your course, but perhaps may include managers you have interviewed or people with whom you have worked. You might also need to consider other researchers or future generations of students reading your work if reports are retained in a library. Considering all these potential readers implies that the project report should be a formal document, aimed at senior, experienced and academic readers whom you do not know well. Thus, it is inappropriate to use slang expressions or to adopt a conversational tone. On the other hand, you do need to tell the whole story, so a little emotion and colour is allowable. However, you should avoid colloquial expressions ('this software is well evil') and short forms (for 'can't' use 'cannot') and avoid jokes or sly asides. Cartoons may be more acceptable, but even they should only be used in moderation. The project report is an academic document and you should avoid hype (e.g. 'such and such technology will change the world') and sales propaganda ('such and such software package has been written by top programmers and tuned to perfection by a quality control procedure second to none').

We would advise you to avoid excessive use of the first person ('I' and 'we') but you should use it for emphasis or where the passive voice becomes awkward. The usual advice is to avoid as far as possible the second person ('you', 'your'). Note however that in this book, since we are offering advice directly to a reader, we do use the second person from time to time and it would be quite awkward if we did not. This raises the particular problem of writing user documentation or manuals to accompany software. If such writing is required as a part of a project, then a direct, active voice style is preferred (Denton and Kelly, 1993).

It is also good practice to handle gender in a sensitive way. Not all people are masculine, indeed, most are not. It is usually possible to avoid gross use of 'he', 'his' and 'him' by substituting plural pronouns. Thus, 'The manager should be trained to use his personal computer' becomes 'Managers should be trained to use their personal computers'. The grammatically correct solution, while retaining the singular subject, is to write 'The manager should be trained to use his or her personal computer', but over-use of this form can make text sound very pedantic. Alternative approaches are to alternate masculine and feminine, or even to make a point by using all feminine pronouns. The use of such neologisms as 's/he', is not a very useful solution.

When writing, try to avoid long sentences; these are tiring to read and can only too easily lose focus. Long sentences are also more likely to contain grammatical errors. Also, do not write single sentence paragraphs. These can make a report seem fragmented and insubstantial.

Beware of overusing abbreviations. If you litter your text with IT, DSS, AI, ESS and MIS then the impression you make will be of a lazy mind at work. At the very least you should spell out the full text the first time you introduce an abbreviation, or even provide a list of abbreviations to be used in the front part of a project report. It is much better to try to avoid them as far as possible; in doing so you will have to think harder about what you really want to say and improve the overall feel of your document. It is also usual to use words to express numbers in the text where the number is less than twenty, or less than a hundred and divisible by ten; e.g. use 'ten, seventeen, ninety, 21, 89, 47, 712'.

Achieving a good sense of style in a document is often a case of being consistent. In matters such as page layout, spelling ('organization' or 'organisation', but not both in the same document), or style of citing references, consistency will convey a confident feeling to your reader. Remember too that consistency in such matters helps the reader to concentrate on and understand your meaning, rather than being irritated by odd surprises.

Use of quotations

Use quotations sparingly. There are only three occasions when you should need to use a quotation:

- where the original author has written something more succinctly, elegantly or clearly than you could ever express it;
- where you need to prove that it was a particular author who wrote the words, or you are introducing some text in order to analyse it in greater detail;
- where there is no reasonable way of paraphrasing, such as when quoting lists or formulae.

On other occasions you should express the idea in your own words and place a reference to the origin. When giving a quotation in the body of your text it is usual to use single quotation marks ' ', though some authorities may recommend the double quote. This is certainly one of those areas in which consistency is the main aim. The other use of quotation marks, to enclose book titles, is largely obsolete now that printers can produce italic text. The single quote can also be used *sparingly* for emphasis, as can an italic font. When quotes are used care should also be taken to select the correct opening and closing quote. Some word-processors will do this automatically, a so-called 'smart quotes' feature. Long quotations, say longer than two or three lines of printed text, should be placed as a separate paragraph, indented and should have no quotation marks.

Words and phrases to use with caution

In addition to common grammatical and stylistic problems, there are also certain difficulties with particular words and phrases due largely to their over-use or abuse over the years. In most cases, we are not suggesting that such words should never be used, but rather we would advise the use of an alternative wherever possible. The words and phrases we would particularly draw attention to are as follows:

etc.
    For giving examples in a list, the phrases 'for example' or 'such as' are preferable.

power, user-friendly, paradigm, model, integrated
    These words have been over-used and abused to the point of losing meaning.

methodology
> Do you really mean method or approach?

philosophy
> Do you really mean approach? For example, client-server is not a philosophy – if in any doubt ask a philosopher.

got, gotten
> Banish these words from your written vocabulary.

clearly, obviously, of course, naturally
> If it is so clear, obvious or natural why do you need to draw attention to it? Also beware of other meaningless modifiers such as basically, virtually, actually, practically.

in other words
> Are you really facilitating an explanation by rephrasing the idea or are you just repeating yourself or trying to change the subject?

many, most, some, a few
> What kind of a claim are you making? Is there evidence to back it?

posit
> When did you ever hear anybody actually say this word, and do you really know what it means? In general it is quite acceptable to replace it with the word 'suggests', 'proposes' or 'puts forward'.

must, will
> In predicting the future behaviour of people, 'may' or 'are likely to' are much less deterministic, as well as more accurate. For example, 'managers are likely to welcome end-user computing' allows for the case where some managers resist it. Similarly, 'the introduction of information technology may improve the organization's productivity' allows for those cases where it has been a disastrous failure.

the fact, in fact
> Is this really a fact or just a convenient supposition?

heretofore, whilst … .
> Avoid antiquated or obsolete words and expressions.

Writer's block

People who are usually confident and proficient writers can at times find themselves stuck and unable to make any progress. This is known as writer's block. If you do come to the point where you feel that writing is impossible, and that you are seriously intimidated by blank pages, then you do need to do something about it. There is no simple solution to this problem, but we can suggest a few ideas that may help.

First, you need to understand why you are blocked. There may be many possible reasons, and these may have nothing to do with the work at hand. For example, it may be because you do not have sufficient understanding of your topic and do not know where to start. In this case it is perhaps right to stop trying to write, and to do a bit more data gathering or analysis. It may equally be that you have too rich an understanding and fear that you will be unable to express it. Some students find that they avoid writing until they have a 'complete' understanding; while questions and doubts are in their mind they will not start to write. In these cases, our recommendation is to start to write explicitly *about* the doubts and confusions. In this way, and through trying to express clearly the things that are causing concern, the writer can often clarify exactly where the problem lies, as a first essential step to its resolution. But even if the uncertainty remains, the exploration of such problematic issues is at the heart of good research. Things that are worthy of research are difficult and complex, and in our writing we need to acknowledge this.

Another technique to overcome hesitancy in starting to write is to move back from writing itself and try to develop stronger structures for your work. This may be in the traditional form of outlines, section headings and key issues to cover, but it may also be achieved by drawing pictures and diagrams. For some people using a white-board and coloured pens can help. If you can achieve a quite detailed breakdown, in whatever manner, then the individual elements that need to be written may be that much smaller and less intimidating.

Talking about the topic may also help. You can talk to your teachers, or talk to your friends, but often it is talking to an uninvolved person that can break down the blockage. Many undergraduate students explain their projects to their puzzled parents, and perhaps the parents are none the wiser at the end, but the act of explaining itself can be very helpful. Another person to talk to is yourself. With a tape recorder it is possible to express a 'stream of consciousness' on the topic with no particular concern as to neat and rational argument. When the tape is replayed, the ideas expressed may be capable of being more formally captured. Some people even find that they can 'talk in sentences and paragraphs', and thus can dictate a text that they would find hard to write at a keyboard.

If you find that you have trouble in starting to write it may be less to do with fundamental questions of understanding of your topic, and more to do with day-to-day preoccupations or distractions. If this is the case then you need to address the root cause. In some cases though, altering some aspect of your writing routine may help. For example, some people need physical stimulation before they can write, perhaps going swimming or running. It may equally be that you need some intellectual stimulation, perhaps going to a film or reading a novel. If these activities can get your brain moving, then you may be able to start work with a more creative and positive attitude. Another answer to mild writer's block is to turn to low level and mundane activities at the word-processor. If you cannot write the difficult introduction to Chapter 3, then you may at least be able to enter some references or to spellcheck Chapter 2.

Charts, diagrams and tables

Some pictures are worth a thousand words, but by no means all. Too many diagrams can result in boring the reader. Hence the diagrams and pictures that are included in a final report should be chosen carefully. In order for the data labels to be clearly legible, it is often necessary to make the chart quite large (often a full page). Before you commit yourself to this, ask yourself whether the chart is necessary: does it say anything, is the relationship that you are depicting sensible?

While charts and tables can convey a lot of information, remember that you are asking your reader to stop reading in order to interpret the chart. Therefore, a chart or diagram needs to be meaningful and important in the context of the argument presented. For example, a chart is normally unnecessary to represent the responses to a question that only has two possible answers; for example, 80 per cent of the respondents said 'yes' and the remaining 20 per cent answered 'no'.

Pie charts, bar charts, histograms, line graphs and (less often) scatter plots are excellent ways of presenting various types of data and, more particularly, showing the relationship between data items. However, such charts are not interchangeable and they should only be used in the appropriate situations. Thus, pie charts are useful when, in some way, the various categories of data sum to a 'whole' (e.g. various manufacturers' shares of the mobile phone market). However, this is often not the case; for example, when you ask respondents for the advantages of a particular technology and the respondents choose more than one answer. In this case a bar chart would be more appropriate. A line graph is suitable for showing some form of quantitative relationship, while scatter plots are useful for demonstrating the distribution of data points measured in two dimensions. For these statistical charts, it is essential to label the axes (where appropriate) and include the scope in the caption; for example, 'the world market for …', 'survey results (n = 100)'. Legends should always be provided to allow the interpretation of shaded areas, for example on a bar chart.

Diagrams and pictures are also useful for depicting many qualitative concepts and notions, not just for quantitative or statistical data. They can be powerful ways of providing clarity and reducing complexity. Among the possible uses are the following:

- Organization charts to represent a management structure.
- Geographical maps/plans to show spatial and organizational aspects.
- System charts to show the way system components interface.
- Conceptual frameworks.
- Rich pictures and mind maps, for example, as used in soft systems methodology.
- The various forms of diagram used in structured systems analysis, for example, data flow diagrams.

Designing tables

Tables can be useful for presenting data; however, care needs to be taken that each table is meaningful, necessary and clear. Tables should take up no more than one page and be oriented (either portrait or landscape) in the way that makes them most readable. Small tables can be included within the main text, larger tables merit a page of their own and are often better presented in landscape format.

Be selective regarding the attributes of a situation or data that you decide to use as columns of a table. Sometimes two small neat tables are preferable to trying to squeeze everything into one large table. Also, think carefully about the ordering of the rows and columns. Arranging rows in descending order of magnitude is often sensible, and columns should be ordered so that appropriate comparisons can be made of the various aspects of the data. Column headings need to be concise yet unambiguous (often a difficult trade-off) and should contain the units, where appropriate. For example, tables look much neater where '%' is shown in the column heading, rather than repeated for every data item. Other formatting aspects, such as column widths, justification (left, centre, decimal), and the use of ruled lines all need to be considered. It may be better not to produce any large tables, rather than producing unattractive, muddled or illogical tables.

All charts, diagrams and tables used in your project research require a caption (or title) and these normally look better placed below the figure or table to which they refer. In published books however, table titles usually go at the top while figure titles go below. Figures and tables should be numbered within sections; for example, Figure 3.1, Table 1.2. Where you have taken a figure from another source, you should show the source in the caption.

There are a number of useful guides that provide further more detailed advice on using graphics to convey information, such as Reynolds and Simmonds (1984) or Tufte (2001).

Structure of a project report

A project report will normally need to contain the elements described below.

Cover with title, author, year and course name

Remember that teachers may have to deal with many project reports, and the student's name, the title of the project and course for which it is submitted should normally appear on the outside front cover. Alternatively, institutions may have anonymous marking conventions, and require that names be removed from project work and substituted with an examination entry number. Many institutions will specify the format and binding, and may even supply the front cover page, and this may include a required statement from you to the effect that the work is yours and yours alone.

Title page with an abstract

Abstracts are usually required, and should be between 100–300 words. An abstract should convey concisely what is in the report and the main arguments it contains. It should contain no citations or other external references. It is good practice to write the final abstract last, remembering that it should encapsulate what is *actually* in the project, not what you wished was in the project or thought might be there some months before. Remember that the purpose of an abstract is to allow somebody to 'preview' the work, and decide if they wish to read it in full, so an abstract should clearly convey the topic, the research approach and the main findings and conclusions. What an abstract is not is an opportunity to recycle the first paragraph of your report! There is a real art to writing good concise abstracts, and it is worthwhile to consult some journals and to critically evaluate the quality of the abstracts that they print at the head of articles.

Acknowledgements

It is often appropriate to acknowledge various people for the help they have given in preparing a project. A well written set of acknowledgements conveys some real information to the examiner, and can emphasize the variety of informal sources that have been used. It may also be the place to thank briefly the cat or your mother.

Contents page

Do not overdo the sections and section numbering. A chapter, which may comprise 10–20 pages, is usefully broken down into sections (e.g. Section 4.2 is the second section of the fourth chapter). A contents page may usefully show this second level of structure, but generally no further levels. The numbering of sub-sections (e.g. 4.2.1 or, worse, 4.2.1.5) normally adds more complexity than clarity and should be avoided. Wordprocessors will do wonderful and totally uninteresting things in the way of indexing and contents pages, but the temptation to produce the ultimate contents page should be resisted. It is however appropriate to include a separate list of tables, illustrations or figures.

The body of the report

This should be organized into sections or chapters and an appropriate structure is discussed in the following section.

References

Project reports require a references section with a full bibliographic record (reference) for all the materials used. Such a full and proper citation will include the full name of all the authors; the full title of the book or article; the title of the journal, if appropriate; place, publisher and date of publication. The only acceptable way to do this is by consistently following a standard style format. Consulting a few academic journals should also help in establishing what a full citation should contain, though close inspection will reveal that journal styles vary somewhat in terms of the detail, order of layout and punctuation. On no account try to invent your own novel method of providing references, the examiners will not be impressed.

All material quoted verbatim, from any source, must be indicated as such, and paraphrases, or ideas, taken from the literature must credit the original source. The usual style within the field of information systems is to give citations within the text, a method known as the Harvard system, and which this book follows: – (Angell and Smithson, 1988) – or 'As described in Cornford and Doukidis (1991), operational research is …'. In this preferred system the author name and date is inserted in the text rather than by the use of numbers in the text [3] or footnotes[1]. You may well find some literature which does use these other systems of referencing, but our strong recommendation is to avoid them. The Harvard system has a number of advantages, and one is that your reader has immediate access to the names of authors and the dates of items used. The full references to all cited works, in the reference section, should then be in alphabetical order and formatted as shown. In this example the references are to first a book, then a government report available on the web, then a chapter within an edited book, and finally to a paper in an academic journal.

Angell, I. O. and S. Smithson (1990) *Information Systems Management: Opportunities and Risks* (London: Macmillan).

Dunleavy, P. and H. Margetts (2002) 'Cultural Barriers to e-government: A report for the Comptroller and Auditor General'. HC 704–111 (London: Stationery Office). Available at (http://www.nao.org.uk/publications/nao_reports/01–02/0102704-iii.pdf). Last accessed 3 March 2005.

Kling, R. (1996) 'Hopes and horrors: technological utopianism and anti-utopianism in narratives of computerization', in R. Kling (ed.) *Computerization and Controversy: Value Conflicts and Social Choices* (San Diego: Academic Press) pp. 40–8.

Straub, D. W. and R. T. Watson (2001) 'Research commentary: Transformational issues in researching IS and net-enabled organizations', *Information Systems Research*, vol. 12, no. 4, pp. 337–45.

The idea behind providing such a full reference is to allow a reader to locate the material in question. In that light, all the items of information included in the citations above are required, right up to the correct page numbers. It is conventional to capitalize all main words in a book's title or a journal's title, but not in the title of an article within a journal. If you use a bibliographic software package, as discussed above, then many of these questions of formatting references and laying out citations will be taken care of once you have mastered the software.

Appendices

An appendix is a place to put peripheral or supporting materials for your project, material whose inclusion in the main body of the text would tend to

---

[1] Footnotes are not the best way to give reference, but they may have other uses; for example, to give some tangential information or to back up a point made.

break the flow of the argument. It will often be appropriate to include the original Project Proposal and project plan plus any detailed documentation generated during the project. For example, in a traditional systems analysis project, it would probably be the case that some of the high-level data flow or use case diagrams would be included in the main body of the report, but the full set of detailed diagrams would be in an appendix. Similarly, any reports produced for a client might be included as an appendix. You should not, however, put any 'essential' material (text, tables or diagrams) in an appendix that a 'normal' reader would absolutely have to refer to.

So far in this chapter we have followed the normal sequence of the materials within a project report in a form which should result in a report that is straightforward to read, but there may be a good reason to vary this a little. For example, in practice it may be better to place the references at the very end and after any appendices. In this way the reader can swiftly find them. It may also be necessary to add other elements, a glossary or list of abbreviations for example. If this is needed then by convention it should come at the front of the report, since it is required preliminary reading.

The body of the report

As a student on a formal course you should have clear guidance as to the expected length of a report; in the case of an undergraduate project perhaps in the region of 6500 to 8000 words, for a Masters student perhaps 10,000 to 12,000 words. Whatever the limit is, you should be clear whether it applies to the whole document, or just to the main body; marks may be deducted for excessive length. If you think that you are exceeding the limit then submit yourself to a heavy course of self-criticism. Are all those words really necessary? Could you not make a greater impact by obliterating extraneous verbosity? Be brief. Come to the point. Do not tell your reader what they already know. In any case, additional (or peripheral) materials are better included as appendices.

In the main body of the report take care to emphasize *your* contribution; for example, 'The interviews undertaken showed that ...'. A prudent but not excessive use of quotes from interviewees or other explanatory material often adds colour to the project even if a full transcript is in an appendix; for example, according to one project manager interviewed:

> This system is appalling. It has cost the company a fortune, ten of my best programmers have resigned and my hair is turning grey.

Introducing lists into a report needs to be handled carefully. Too many lists make a project report appear boring and mechanical and give a sense of work half done. It often makes sense to place lists as figures and then to discuss their contents in the main text. Where lists are long, say more than twelve items, try to group the items in some way. For example, 'organizational problems' and 'technical problems' might be used to structure a list of general problems found in a study of a particular system. It is normally pointless to number the items in such a list, unless they are going to be referred to by that number in the body of the text.

The main body of the report should be organized into chapters in the following manner, though this is just a baseline description and particular projects may require different approaches. If you do deviate from this suggested structure, for example, if you have undertaken a software engineering project and are following a style recommended for such projects, then you should be quite clear in your own mind why you are doing so. Some projects may have a 'natural' structure that is distinctive but, whatever structure you use, you should be sure to cover the main points discussed below. Most of all you should remember that the project report needs to 'tell a story' and thus needs a beginning, a middle and an end.

Chapter 1 – The introduction

By definition, this should introduce the project to the reader; in other words, the reader should be given information as to the content and structure of the report, as well as some motivation to read it. Thus, it is necessary to describe briefly what the project is about: the project's scope and to emphasize why it is an interesting and important topic. The introduction should also include a 'plan' (or road-map) of the project; for example, 'Chapter 2 provides an overview of the objectives of this study … Chapter 3 discusses …' (see Box 9.1 for key points to be alert to when writing projects).

BOX 9.1

Key points to keep in mind in writing up projects

- Know your reader
- Write to tell a story, with a beginning, middle and an end
- Exploit the wordprocessor and appropriate tools (bibliography program, spelling checkers, drawing programs), but don't become a slave to them
- Take care with grammar and use of language. Bad grammar will suggest to your reader a lack of care in undertaking the work
- Write in order to inform, not to dazzle. Beware of excess, including excessive use of quotations, charts, tables or fonts.

Chapter 2 – Literature review

This chapter is where you demonstrate your knowledge of the area and locate your work in the context of the rest of the literature. Ideally your research question should emerge from this discussion (or be justified in greater detail) as a gap or conflict in the literature. For example, you may find that electronic banking has been researched a lot in the USA and Western Europe but it may not have been investigated in your home country. This is a gap in the literature that you can fill. A conflict may exist between two alternative theories, or between prediction and fact. An example of the latter is that a few years ago commentators in the UK were predicting that mobile commerce (m-commerce) would grow significantly but, at the time of writing (2005), this has not been the case. Similarly many people for many years have predicted an explosion of technology-based home working (telework), but this too has not really taken off to the degree predicted. Here we have conflicts that ask to be researched and perhaps resolved.

For most projects, it is essential to review the existing literature as it forms the academic context of the project. This allows you to introduce and discuss the theories and concepts that you use, as well as those you have rejected. The review of the literature allows the reader to see where your work fits and also the extent of your contribution. Care should be taken to ensure that the review is directed towards the specific topic area and the themes of the project and is not just a general 'textbook' review of a wider field.

Chapter 3 – The objectives of the project and the methods used to achieve them

In this chapter you should clearly set out, against the background of the surveyed literature, the objectives of this project and the methods used. Briefly summarize the approach taken (e.g. structured systems analysis, object-oriented design and programming, a case study based on semi-structured interviews, a postal questionnaire) and any initial assumptions that you made. A project will be judged in part on the coherence and clarity of these objectives and the appropriateness of the methods selected. This latter point will almost always require that a range of possibilities are introduced and assessed before the chosen approach is described in more detail.

Chapter 4 – Conceptual framework

This chapter should present (with references to relevant literature) the theory or conceptual framework that you have adopted and justify that choice.

In this chapter you will need to describe in some detail the 'concepts' that you are working with and the relationships between them. As a simple example (too simple), consider a study of IS strategy and competitive advantage which takes Michael Porter's 5 forces model as its framework of analysis. This suggests a number of concepts to be worked with (e.g. industry structure, competitor, substitute goods, supplier). As another example, a study of knowledge management might take the distinction between tacit and explicit knowledge and the SECI process, as described by Nonaka and Takeuchi (1995) and used by many authors since.

Chapter 5 – Findings

In this chapter you should present an edited but relatively un-interpreted description of the results of your empirical work (e.g. observations, interviews, questionnaire data). In other words, show the reader what you found out from the empirical side of the work. You should not overwhelm the reader with entire interview transcripts or frequency distributions for every question on a questionnaire. The trick is to edit out the uninteresting or inconclusive items (these might be dropped off into an appendix) and focus on the main story. However, at this stage, do not over 'interpret' your findings. This normally comes in the next chapter. The difficult balance in a findings chapter is to discover a useful way of presenting your work. It could be in temporal terms (this and then that), it could be by theme (views of management, views of customers). It could be in terms of your framework presented in the previous chapter, but if so, try not to pre-judge your analysis.

Chapter 6 – Analysis

Research is about collecting and displaying data but equally important is the analysis and interpretation of that data. This is where you offer and justify your own interpretation of what has been observed or achieved. It is important that this discussion relates back to the objectives of the project and to the theoretical aspects covered in the literature review. Care should be taken that the analysis and discussion are presented in a well-structured and logical fashion.

Here you apply your particular theory or conceptual framework to the empirical data in order to discuss: 'what it all means' and/or 'why things are the way they are'. Try to do this through balanced argument (and not evangelical preaching). Normally situations are not entirely black or white and so, even if you are in favour of the technology or system under investigation, you should also point out any problems or drawbacks. This is probably the most difficult chapter to write, as this is where you are bringing together theory and practice. However, if you do it well, you are likely to score highly.

Chapter 7 – Conclusion

There are two main aspects of the work that you need to include here. The first is a summary or assessment of the work itself: what have you achieved, what have you discovered, what further lines of activities do you see as leading from here? Emphasize here the main findings, perhaps with any obvious limitations, and claim your contribution. You also may feel that you wish to make some relevant recommendations for practice or suggest ideas for future research.

The second aspect that the examiners are looking for in the last sections is your own assessment of how well you handled the project: what did you learn yourself, what do you now wish you had done differently? Do not be embarrassed to point out your errors or to highlight the weaker aspects of your work. The examiners are interested in what you have learned from undertaking the project, as much as with the actual result.

Questions of layout

There are still some details of presentation that we need to address. The generic structure given above, revised to fit in your particular project, can provide a good basic template for the substance of your report, but its impact and readability can still be enhanced by careful attention to presentation.

You need to aim for a pleasing layout, avoiding any impression of 'wide open spaces' or an excessive concern for rainforests by squashing the material too much. Do not use enormous margins; 2.5 cm or 1 inch all around is appropriate, any more starts to look too empty on the page. Use a serif font such as Times Roman for your main text. You may wish to use a san-serif font such as Helvetica for the headings. Beyond this basic choice beware of 'fontitis'. This is an unpleasant disease that puts readers off. No reader wishes to see examples of all the fonts supported by your software (especially not on the same page). Equally, on no account print large blocks of text in italic or bold fonts; this just makes them very hard to read. Use a reasonable size of font – generally 11 or 12-point for the main text. Any smaller may make reading difficult and any larger tends to look wasteful and a bit childish.

Work should usually be presented in a single column format and fully justified. Use 1.5 or double line spacing and leave one blank line between paragraphs. Most institutions expect work to be printed as single-sided documents. While laser printers and wordprocessing software will now support double-sided printing, in practice, and with the usual binding techniques, double-sided documents are hard to read.

Use standard white paper (A4 size or similar) for the text; large diagrams may go into the report as a fold-out. It is usually not a good idea to print your report on extra thick paper so as to generate a feeling of bulk, or to use coloured paper for a designer effect. The result may well be a feeling of all style and no content. All copies of a project should be presented in secure bindings. Nothing is more annoying to examiners than projects that fall apart. For this reason, ring binders are often unacceptable, and in any event they are very bulky to store and handle.

Summary of layout guidelines

Font	Times Roman or similar serif font
Font Size	11 or 12 point
Line spacing	1.5 or 2 line spacing
Quotations	Use single line spacing and indent block quotations
Paper size	A4 or similar, use regular paper and not coloured paper or card
Justification	Use full justification
Header	No headers
Footers	Page number at bottom centre
Widow/orphan	Switch on widow/orphan control in your word processor and monitor layout carefully
Page numbers	Place the page number at the bottom centre of the page
Margins	1 inch (2.54 cm) on all sides
Chapter and section headings	Use Bold and 14 point for main headings, and just bold for lesser headings. You may vary the font in headings – for example Ariel
Footnotes	Use sparingly, if at all, and never for references
Colour printing	Use only if *really* needed
Paragraphs	Use a blank line to mark the start of paragraphs

Each chapter of your report should start on a new page. Chapter headings should be in bold, centred and in a large font, section headings should be in bold and left-justified. If you need a third level of headings then use italics. With laser printers, upper case headings and underlining do not normally look attractive.

Number chapters, and perhaps the sections within them too if you wish, but do not number paragraphs or sub-sections. Place page numbers on the bottom of the page and centre them. Running headers or footers at the top or bottom of the page can be attractive, as long as they are not too obtrusive.

Try hard to avoid 'widows' and 'orphans' – single short lines of text left on the wrong page. Be particularly careful to avoid headings at the foot of pages. Note, however, that dealing with such problems is best left until quite late in the production of a report since small changes in text will inevitably alter layout significantly. Thus it makes sense to do the detailed layout work at the end of a project period – but time must be allowed for this work.

Take care to position figures, diagrams and tables for easy reference when reading the text and follow good practice for appropriate labelling, never forgetting to clarify units of measure or scales. Take particular care regarding the position, size and legibility of tables and diagrams if they have been 'resized' to fit into the text.

The overall effect that you should aim for is a report that is clean and business like and that attracts the reader. Too many fancy effects will detract from your work and convey a feeling of confusion. So too will an over bulky feel to your report.

No matter how good the basic ideas of the research study, if the project report is badly written or poorly presented, these ideas are likely to be lost to the reader/examiner. We have seen many projects where good data and innovative analysis have been spoiled by shoddy presentation and appalling writing style. Good writing cannot make up for lack of content, but it can present the content in the best possible light. Therefore, it is important to consider carefully the writing style, structure and presentation of the report.

Making a presentation

As part of the assessment process, students may have to make an oral presentation of their projects. Typically, they are given 15–20 minutes to present, with a little time allowed for questions. This is especially the case where part of the project involves the production of software, in which case much of the presentation would be a demonstration of the software. Viva examinations for PhD or research Masters degrees are slightly different, but some of the following suggestions apply to any type of presentation of research work.

Like the writing of reports, the ability to make a good presentation is a very useful skill that is frequently needed in a wide range of jobs. Certain jobs (e.g. consultants, academics and politicians) involve making presentations of some sort on almost a daily basis but most managers need such skills regularly; for example, in presenting proposals to meetings. While public speaking seems to come naturally for some people, the majority can learn how to prepare and deliver an effective presentation through a little thought and practice.

Preparation

Even the most experienced public speaker will advise you that the secret of a good presentation is good preparation (see Box 9.2). No matter how good the speaker is at delivery, if the content is poor then the presentation will fail. Preparation involves two related issues: first, deciding what to present and, second, how to present it. Special care should be taken in selecting the content (the 'what' to present); it is impossible to present all 10,000 words of a project report in twenty minutes. Don't try! You clearly need to summarize the research, compressing the main points into the time allowed, but without losing too much of value. We offer the following key aspects to keep in mind.

First, you need to know your audience and know what they expect from you. Be careful not to just tell them what they already know, but instead try to link your material to their existing knowledge. Think about the structure of your presentation. Just as with a report, a presentation should have a beginning (an introduction), a middle (the main body) and an end (the conclusion). This will involve: 'saying what you are going to say', 'saying it' and finally 'saying what you said'. Furthermore, the main body should flow in a logical fashion and not resemble a random walk.

Take care to emphasize the interesting parts of your work and avoid basic material or the incomprehensible. It may not always be easy to decide what is interesting, but you should try to avoid areas that you do not really understand. Some advice from your adviser may help here. When presenting try to maintain a consistent level of information for your audience. In other words,

---

BOX 9.2

Key considerations when preparing presentations

- To present well you need to prepare in advance.
- Think about your audience, what do they want to hear?
- Concentrate on the interesting parts of your work.
- Plan your use of visual aids and be realistic in their number and content.
- Consider providing a brief handout to amplify the detail of your work.

do not go into tremendous detail on particular points and skim over others. If the audience is interested, and need further information, they can ask for fine detail in their questions at the end.

You need to be prepared for questions. Consider (and prepare for) likely questions; these may refer to the relevance or generalizability of your work, the methodology you adopted, or how your work is linked to the literature. Where appropriate, you should take into consideration any other presentations being given on the same day. Try not to duplicate them, but instead try to link your presentation to the others.

Using visual aids

Having decided what material to present, the next question to address is how to present it. In most cases, this involves the use of overhead transparencies or presentation software such as Powerpoint. In preparing slides, whether printed out or projected from a computer, we would suggest that you pay attention to the following points.

Ration the number of slides. The average time needed to explain each 'content bearing' slide is around four to five minutes, depending upon their information content. This implies the use of no more than five 'main' slides in a twenty-minute presentation. Yet we have seen students arrive for a ten-minute presentation with no fewer than 30 slides; clearly an impossible task, and the beginning of an embarrassing fiasco.

Each slide should say something but not everything – it should hold the audiences attention but not substitute for what you are going to say. In other words, each slide should have a particular function or deal with a specific part of the research. Slides should be readable from where the audience is sitting. Avoid large blocks of text on slides and use 'bullets' to provide structure and emphasis. It is also important to select a large enough font for projected text (minimum 24 point) and certainly it is not appropriate to reproduce complex diagrams or tables directly from a report; they just become unreadable. If thought through from the beginning, diagrams can be very helpful, but extraneous artwork – sometimes n our experience verging on the psychedelic – should be avoided and that includes too much animation of slides. It may be a good idea to support your slides with a 'hand-out'. This can help overcome the problem of delivering complex diagrams, as well as giving the audience something that they can retain for future reference.

Try to make the slides attractive and consistent in format. This involves considering issues of fonts and overall layout. Presentation software can provide good models of consistent formats, and allow you to review alternative formats for the same basic text.

Giving the presentation

For most people, the prospect of any form of public speaking is nerve-wracking, especially where there is some element of assessment involved or the presentation is to a relatively senior or important audience. Even experienced speakers suffer from nerves before major presentations and you just have to build up sufficient confidence in yourself and your material to overcome the 'butterflies in the stomach'. If you have done a reasonable job of your research project, you are the expert and should be able to give a convincing performance. Gaining experience in giving presentations is important. If you are going to be required to do this as part of your project work, then take every opportunity to practise public speaking that comes your way and take note of key considerations given in Box 9.3.

When you are presenting your work take care with timing. Many presentations fail because the presenter loses track of time, often spending far too long on the early sections and then either having to rush the (important) later sections or incurring everyone's displeasure by over-running their time slot. Keep one eye on the clock; it is also helpful to have marked the halfway point in the material so that you can see early on whether you need to speed up or slow down. You might also ask the person chairing the presentation to warn you five minutes before your time is over, and allow you to complete the presentation smoothly. Practice runs in advance can also help determine the likelihood of over-running.

When presenting your work try to be yourself and to be as relaxed and natural as possible (without becoming slovenly). You must be sure to face the

---

BOX 9.3

Key considerations when making a presentation

- Remember, you are the expert, and have something to say.
- Gain experience in public speaking and rehearse your talk in advance.
- Take care with timing and make sure that the main message is delivered in the early parts of a talk.
- Speak slowly and clearly, addressing the back of the room while making eye contact with your audience.
- When presenting do your best to keep your body still, this will give a calm and confident message to the audience.
- Answer questions directly and briefly. Do not get into arguments or take exception to pointed questions.

audience and to speak slowly and clearly to the person in the back row – this should ensure that your voice carries sufficiently without any sense of your shouting at the audience. It is also important to maintain eye contact with the people you are talking to. The audience may not be particularly attractive but you must look at them, rather than turning your back or peering at the screen, the slides or some obscure spot on the ceiling.

Our advice to students in presenting their work is that they should talk, not read. Believe it or not, this advice is *particularly* relevant for students who are not native English speakers. If you know your subject, you will get it across to the audience in some way or other, and you have no problems of spelling or fine details of grammar to worry about either. In an aural presentation the audience does not expect perfect sentences and paragraphs. Even a confident native English speaker, when presenting, will mangle sentences, shift verb tenses and 'um and err' at times. If you do read a prepared text, it tends to sound unconvincing, second hand, or disconnected from the speaker. At worst it can sound as though you have no idea what you are saying!

The slides you prepare should give you a general structure to follow, and from there you need to explain your material in your own words. Just as you should not read from a prepared text, don't read from the slides. If you think you may forget something important, and it is not on the slides, then use a limited number of prompt cards with *brief* text (key ideas) on them.

As you present, work through the slides systematically. If you are working from printed slides it is very easy to mix them up, especially when someone from the audience asks you to return to an earlier slide. It helps if you keep the 'used' slides in order in a separate pile. It is also a good idea to number slides so that they can be resorted into the correct order if need be.

Try to give a friendly and confident impression. A little humour or an occasional joke may help but jokes should be few and far between, relevant to the material and (at least mildly) amusing. Do not overdo the humour, you are not auditioning for the part of a stand-up comic; if in doubt, 'play it straight'. To create a confident impression you also need to control your arms and legs. Apart from the occasional point of emphasis, arms and legs are not terribly useful in presentations, so try to keep them at bay. Do not walk around. Similarly, avoid jangling your keys or loose change, stroking your ear or entangling yourself in the overhead projector. If you are so nervous that you cannot hold a glass steadily, then avoid glasses of water. Remember also that when a presenter is chewing gum with gusto, it tends to make the audience feel either sick or hungry; neither of which is helpful.

When the time comes, answer as honestly as you can any questions that are asked. You must maintain sufficient energy and concentration to be able to deal with questions at the end of the presentation. If you know the answer to a 'factual' question, give it clearly and politely; do not treat questioners as if they are inattentive buffoons or sadistic inquisitors. If you do not know the answer, then it is normally safest to admit your ignorance, while perhaps pointing to a related area that you did cover properly. Where the issue raised is more subjective, or based on interpretation or opinion, then answer it in the same spirit. Certainly avoid heated arguments but, on the other hand, do not let questioners 'walk all over you' and negate your research.

Summary

- Writing is a skill that we can all hope to improve at. This means that we need to take it seriously and work at our identified problems.
- Exploit the computer tools that are available, but remember that they are not the whole answer to good writing.
- Take time to refresh your knowledge of English grammar and punctuation conventions. Make a list of your worst failings in written English, and work to eliminate the identified errors.
- Think through the structure of your final report. Know where each element of your work will be reported.
- Take care with the details of layout and format. They are an important way to pass a message of careful and thoughtful research.
- For successful presentations, preparation is the key.

Further reading

Summers (1999) is a slim book aimed at all sorts of writers, and includes chapters on writing letters, essays, journals and reports. The book provides a lot of simple advice on grammar, vocabulary and punctuation. Newby (1989) (cited earlier) provides a great deal of useful advice on getting set up for writing, as well as the usual coverage of matters such as spelling and punctuation. Becker (1986) provides a somewhat similar account of the writing process from an American perspective.

The Economist Style Guide (2003) provides brief, alphabetically organized information on many facets of writing style. Some of the information relates to issues of grammar and punctuation but, for the most part, it provides useful information on how to write, spell and describe the world.

Gowers (2002) is a classic work, first produced in 1948 for the benefit of the British Civil Service. The book provides many examples of poor writing, and discusses how to improve them. It also covers the usual matters of grammar and punctuation, as well as providing a checklist of words and phrases to be used with care. Turabian (1996), cited in the references above, is a very well known American text, based on the extensive University of Chicago style guide. You should be able to find a copy in any good library. The level of detail this book contains is breathtaking – how should you make a footnote reference to the United States constitution – but it just might give you the definitive answer to some niggling problem.

Denton and Kelly (1993) is also cited in the references above and would be particularly useful to a student concerned with documenting a computer application or writing user manuals. The book includes much general good advice on writing technical materials, including a good section on what to do when you are stuck. Since it is concerned with writing technical documentation, the authors have a rather different approach to that of most 'essay writing' guides. They see writing a document as a project, needing a clear project management framework with a work breakdown structure and clear milestones along the way.

Becker, H. S. (1986) *Writing for Social Scientists: How to Start and Finish Your Thesis, Book, or Article* (Chicago: University of Chicago Press).

The Economist. (2003) *The Economist Style Guide* (London: The Economist Business Books).

Gowers, E. (2002) *The Complete Plain Words*, third edition (London: Penguin).

Summers, V. (1999) *Clear English* (London: Penguin).

Web resources

EndNote and *ProCite* www.endnote.com www.procite.com

References

Denton, L. and J. Kelly (1993) *Designing, Writing and Producing Computer Documentation* (New York: McGraw-Hill).

Newby, M. (1989) *Writing: A Guide for Students* (Cambridge: Cambridge University Press).

Nonaka, I. and H. Takeuchi (1995) *The Knowledge Creating Company* (Oxford: OUP).

Reynolds, L. and D. Simmonds (1984) *Presentation of Data in Science* (Dordrecht, Netherlands: Nijhoff).

Tufte, E. R. (2001) *The Visual Display of Quantitative Information* (Cheshire, Connecticut: Graphics Press).

Turabian, K. (1996) *A Manual for Writers of Research Papers, Theses and Dissertations* (London: Heinemann).

10 Conclusion

■ **Qualities looked for in a project**
■ **Factors leading to poor marks**
■ **Doing something more with your work**
■ **Final words**

This final chapter discusses the last stages of the research project process, the assessment of the work. Most students and many teachers regard the marking or assessment of the project report as the final 'wrap-up'. In the first section of this chapter we discuss the qualities that examiners typically look for in any project that they are marking. The exact weighting of the criteria varies between courses and institutions but, in our experience, the criteria discussed here are widely used and reflect the expectations of most courses. However, the assessment process need not signify the absolute end of the project and in this chapter we briefly examine some of the opportunities available to take (good) projects a little further.

Qualities looked for in a project

Your project is supposed to be a professionally produced piece of work, intended to demonstrate mastery of some aspect of the discipline of information systems. As such, students should expect to be judged primarily on the quality of their ideas, their ability to sustain the work, and the use of appropriate methods and techniques. All this will be judged for the most part on the basis of the written report that the student submits.

Students need to remember that a good 'business report' may not make a good academic project, at least not without supporting material that relates the 'company report' to relevant information systems ideas. Similarly, as noted in Chapter 9, 'management guides', 'software reviews', 'textbooks' and works of science fiction have their own particular markets, but they are different from that of research projects.

Overall, in undertaking a project, a student should try to meet a mix of the following criteria.

An understanding of information systems

A project needs to demonstrate an appreciation of the interaction of information technology with a business, organizational or social context. This means balancing the technical and non-technical aspects of a research situation and blending them into an emergent whole. Information systems examiners are unlikely to look kindly on a software engineering project that is not firmly rooted in its organizational context, nor will they smile upon an accounting or marketing project that only peripherally mentions information systems. As we argued in Chapter 2, information systems is a complex and varied area of study, and there is ample opportunity to develop project research that shows a clear concern for the field.

An appreciation of research methodology

Examiners will normally look for an awareness of methodological issues. To assess this they may look for some discussions of the following issues in your project report: consideration of alternative approaches or designs for your research project; a reasoned case for the selection of the final research design; and a consideration of issues such as bias, representativeness and verifiability. Chapter 3 provides a discussion of some aspects of research methodology, and can provide a beginning for such work.

Addressing such questions will require you to step outside your project and be self-critical regarding the approach and methods that you use. Students who can reflect on their work, and can place it within current debates on research methodology usually impress examiners. Indeed, it is often a requirement for project work that it should contain a separate section that provides some reflective comments on the work, how it was done and what has been learned.

Project scope and feasibility

Your project report will need to carefully describe the scope of the project and demonstrate the feasibility of the work within the project constraints.

You need to show that you made a wise choice of topic based on careful reflection. Good projects are normally built on such solid foundations and identifying a 'good' problem to investigate, elucidate or solve is a key first step. Chapter 4 offers some guidance on developing project ideas and refining them into a form which will give you confidence in the feasibility of your project and will help you satisfy this criterion. Most research could be improved if more time and resources were available, but a good project report explains how the inevitable trade-offs were made.

Your project will inevitably be less satisfying to the reader if it is evidently a hastily cut-down version of an over-ambitious project that should never have been started. Similarly, experienced readers can soon detect projects that were initially too narrow and the student has had to stitch on extra segments in an *ad hoc* manner in order to produce sufficient 'weight'.

Project management

Examiners will reward students who bring a substantial research project all the way from an initial idea to a satisfactory close. This implies a concern for the management of all the various activities undertaken, including planning, research design, data collection, analysis and final presentation. Chapter 5 provides many hints for such successful project management. Indeed, good project management normally shows strongly in the final report through a feeling that the writer was in control of the process from start to finish. Equally, poor project management will be shown in a sense of chaos and even panic.

Familiarity with the literature

All research projects need to demonstrate their links with existing knowledge in the topic area and this can only be shown by first presenting a good understanding of the important and widely cited literature relevant to the topic. In this way you can demonstrate your grasp of existing theories and show your academic or theoretical starting point for the research. Preparing and presenting a literature review is discussed in Chapter 6.

Many examiners will turn first to the list of references at the end of a project in order to get a flavour of the work. If this list is skimpy, out of date, or plainly irrelevant, you will lose marks. However, it is not enough just to list relevant references, you must also demonstrate that you appreciate how they link together to form a supporting intellectual structure for your work.

Data collection

Most research projects involve the collection of some form of data. This may be through surveys, interviews, case studies or other means. Chapter 7 examines the most common methods of data collection and provides some guidelines for using these methods in practice.

Good projects are normally based on solid data collection where the data is evidently relevant, valid and encompassing. They are also marked by a realistic awareness of the limits of any particular data collection method, and the necessary caution that needs to be exercised in using data. Poor projects, on the other hand, feature data from ambiguous and poorly designed research strategies; for example, a questionnaire that achieves a miserable response rate or from a case study that has little relation with the problem in hand but where access was easy to obtain.

Logical analysis, well-structured arguments, critical evaluation, insightful interpretation and valid generalization

All the criteria discussed above are necessary but they are not sufficient for a 'good' project; for this there needs to be a coherent process of analysis apparent. Most of the previous criteria refer to the building blocks of a project, where competence is essential but which can only provide the framework for the key message or contribution of the project. It is normally through careful analysis that students can demonstrate that they have really 'got on top of' the project topic and extracted the richest meaning or essence from their work.

This is demonstrated where the data collected are related to the objectives of the project and the existing literature, and this synthesis produces new knowledge or confirms earlier hypotheses. Here, students have the opportunity to reveal their talents in analysing data in a logical or carefully considered fashion, and in structuring arguments based firmly on the evidence in hand.

A good project report takes the opportunity to weigh up the evidence presented and to use it in a critical fashion, with the criticism being aimed both at existing orthodoxy and at the student's own efforts. Finally, through the quality of a project's analysis, students have the chance to demonstrate their ability to generalize their findings, though usually from a limited sample or partial view of the world.

To achieve a strong sense of analysis requires particular talents of the intellect which are difficult, if not impossible, to teach. They can however be learned by careful practice. In Chapter 8 we have attempted to provide some advice that should prevent some of the worse errors and may help some latent talents to appear.

Clear and attractive presentation

The overall style, layout and packaging of the project report, as described in Chapter 9, is an area where most students could improve with relatively little effort. The tools are available in most colleges for the production of visually pleasing and highly readable reports, but these tools do need to be used with some care and skill in order to reap the greatest benefit from them. It is safe to assume that your readers enjoy reading and will appreciate a well-produced report. It is equally safe to assume that your readers will be irritated by a turgidly written, sloppily produced report in poor English.

Factors leading to poor marks

We have described above an ambitious list of criteria, and you may not feel that you are able to meet all of them to a high level, but projects will in all probability be marked down if they

- Make no connection between the work presented and the various theories and methods of information systems;
- Are longwinded, tortuous, ill-structured or otherwise difficult to read;
- Do not make clear the sources of evidence used, or use sources uncritically;
- Are full of generalizations without supporting evidence or argument;
- Fail to draw useful conclusions;
- Lack any feeling of perception, logic, coherence or balance.

Furthermore, a project may be marked down, or even rejected, if the use of English is poor, while copying of substantial parts of a report from other people's work will most probably be grounds for failure. Indeed, to copy or pass off elements of other works without giving any citation as to the source, in other words plagiarism, is a most unacceptable practice and excites extreme reaction in most examiners. It certainly should lead to a project being failed. If, at any time, in putting together a project report, you have any doubts concerning your use of quotations or citations, or feel that you may be paraphrasing too closely some other author's work, you should re-read the relevant section in Chapter 9 and seek further guidance.

Marking schemes

A project report will be assessed by examiners by use of a variety of criteria. Some elements of a marking scheme may include the following:

Understanding: Quite a large part of the value of a final grade will be based on mastery of the subject or problem area. This will include such aspects as awareness of the state-of-the-art, knowledge of relevant literature and other sources of information and a critical appreciation of the sources used, as well as the presentation of ideas with logic, coherence and perception. When projects are undertaken outside the university, then understanding will extend to describing and appreciating the organizational context and the nature of the situation studied.

Contribution: There must be a general expectation that the work reported in a research project will make a contribution to our understanding of information systems. This might consist of clarifying ideas, synthesizing material from different sources, identifying worthwhile problems, or drawing valuable conclusions and providing good recommendations. Contribution also means that a project says something, passes on a message or states a distinctive and well argued point of view. As explained in the opening chapter of this book, it should be within the reach of any student in higher education undertaking a project in information systems to produce work that can be read with interest by their teachers.

That said, students working below the PhD level cannot be required to present substantially original research or particularly new or novel ideas – though some do. But, in presenting a project, a student should be able to answer the basic question, 'What would somebody learn from reading my project that they could not learn from a standard textbook?' A practical project can score highly under this heading, just as well as one that is more theoretical, if it shows a well-judged use of the tools and methods of information systems.

Presentation: The style, arrangement of material, clarity of expression and overall presentation is worth marks. Certainly poor presentation detracts from the ability to be convincing about the level of understanding and contribution.

Originality: How do you get the very best marks for a project? This probably requires an elusive additional ingredient, *originality*. Originality, however, should not be confused with the merely novel or the frankly bizarre, outlandish or grotesque.

Doing something more with your work

If you have finished a project, obtained a degree and left the university, then you probably will put your project report in the cupboard, thank your adviser, and never think about it again. Then again, you may not.

You may feel that the work undertaken deserves a wider audience than the examiners. At the very least such work should be retained within the institution for the benefit of students in future years. Good project reports are repositories of ideas and information, adapted to the perspective and style of the institution and ready to be used in future research projects. Many students also wish to review past projects in the early stages of their own work in order to confirm or adjust their expectations of what is required. Equally, it may be that those who have participated in the research, as providers of information or by allowing access to the researcher, may desire to see a version of the work. This has been touched on in Chapter 4 where relationships with a client are discussed. It may also be the case that departments maintain their own research report or working paper series in which a version of a student's projects can be included. We talk of 'a version' because it is probably not appropriate for the whole report to appear in such a series, and herein lies a larger problem. A project report is normally written to satisfy the requirements of a given course, and may not be suitable for other purposes.

Academic journal articles

Beyond these possible outlets, there is the more challenging possibility of preparing some form of paper, perhaps for publication in an academic journal. In Britain at least, the pressure on academics and academic departments to maintain a publication profile is now intense. Publication rates are monitored and feed directly into the funding procedures for universities. A student who wishes to produce a publication out of his or her project, either alone or jointly with their adviser, will therefore normally be encouraged in such a venture. It is certainly appropriate that an adviser should be invited to jointly author an article, particularly where they have provided non-trivial support; they also should have more of the necessary skills to take a piece of work forward through the procedures that lead to publication.

It is important not to underestimate the scale of the task that is implied by turning project work into a published paper in a respected journal. First there is the problem of time and motivation. A student who has finished a project may well be exhausted by the work, and will almost certainly be concerned primarily with what the future holds, not repackaging or developing past work. This leads to the second problem, which is understanding the distinctive qualities that make a piece of work acceptable to a journal.

One solution may be to start out with the possibility of a journal article in mind, and to work towards this as a main goal of the project itself. This would be particularly appropriate within an MSc course for a student who intends to go on to PhD work or who has ambitions for an academic career and it should certainly be in the minds of PhD students. For MSc students, it may be very acceptable within an institution for a project to be presented in the form of such an article, perhaps supported by further appropriate materials.

When a journal article is being prepared it is important to understand the qualities that are looked for by journal editors, and the procedures that articles go through on their way to publication. An academic journal is intended for the dissemination of new insights, understandings or findings. As such, editors try not to publish work that is derivative, purely descriptive or of little interest to others; yet a project report may quite justifiably contain just such material. Journal articles are expected to get directly to a point, and that point should be one of significant interest to the journal's readers. This also indicates that the choice of which journal to submit an article to is important. There may be no point in sending an article extolling a soft systems view of requirements analysis to a theoretical software engineering journal, or an interpretive case study to a journal with a reputation for publishing quantitative research. It is also important to recognize the prestige order of journals, some are seen as much more prominent in their field, and their standards may be in some sense higher. At the very least, there will be more competition to have an article published in such journals.

When you have selected a suitable journal for your work, take care to discover the correct format for a submission. Most journals publish a page of 'instructions to authors', and it is worth studying this carefully. It will tell you such things as how many copies are required and to whom they should be sent, as well as detailed information about the length of abstract required or the format of references expected.

All journal articles normally go through a refereeing process; that is, they are sent to acknowledged authorities in the field, and these people are asked to comment on the manuscript. It is usual for this to be a double-blind process; the author does not know the names of the referees, and the referees do not know the names of the authors. At least two referees are usually chosen by a journal editor and the main question that they are asked is: 'Should we publish this?' Their answer may be equally direct: 'no', or even 'yes'. However, it may be the case, indeed it usually is, that the referees are less definite. They say that the article is interesting, potentially useful, but … . Suggestions then follow in terms of comments on the article's originality and interest level, its basis in the supporting literature, the use of methods and techniques, the structure and writing style and so on. Even so, these comments will be brief, usually less than one page.

Assuming that an article does not get a direct rejection, it is then passed back to the authors with the referees' comments and with the implied invitation to rewrite. This first cycle, from submission to return of referees' comments will take time, perhaps a minimum of two months, and quite probably six. A rewritten or revised paper will have to re-enter the cycle, and so it all takes time, time during which enthusiasm may wane. A brief look at the timing footnotes that many journals append to articles will confirm these gloomy facts.

Conference presentations

The length of time that it takes to get a journal article published may suggest that another route should be considered in order to find an audience, such as an academic conference. There are normally plenty of conferences, ranging from the very specialized to the most general and all embracing. There are also conferences held in warm places with beaches and palm trees – Paris in springtime, New Orleans at Mardi Gras. Some journals and academic society newsletters publish regular lists of forthcoming conferences and ISWorld Net can offer a comprehensive listing.

One advantage of submitting a paper to a conference rather than a journal is that the time-scale is substantially compressed. From the call for papers or announcement of a conference to the event itself is seldom more than a year, and may be just a few months. The procedures for submitting papers to conferences vary considerably. Some conferences just require a brief abstract of a presentation to be submitted, and only require that the authors attend and present their work, often in a time slot of no more than half an hour. More established conferences may require the submission of full papers, have a formal reviewing or refereeing process, and publish papers in a book of conference proceedings. Such proceedings may be a desk-top published volume only available for participants, but they may be published by an established scientific publisher or made available online. In this case a conference paper can find its way into the reference literature of the discipline.

Conferences also have the important attribute of bringing the participants together, and allowing people to meet and engage in informal discussion and debate. For any person with ambitions for an academic career, attendance at conferences is an essential activity for these reasons if for no others. However, before deciding whether to submit a version of your work for those interesting conferences that you have found in Sydney and Rio de Janeiro, you must face up to the fact that academic conference organizers do not pay any of the expenses of conference participants, even those presenting papers. Indeed, they expect a participation fee from you!

Final words

Carrying out an information systems research project should be a worthwhile, creative and enjoyable experience for both students and their advisers. In most cases, students can learn much more from such a process of creative enquiry than from dreary lectures or the stressful lottery of examinations. Students can take away from the process a sense of achievement at having identified a real problem and either solved it or gone somes way towards providing a sophisticated understanding. Furthermore, this process has been recorded in a well-produced project report, which is something tangible that can be shown to potential employers and shared with other researchers in the same area.

As we have described throughout this book, there are many pitfalls along the way to carrying out such a project successfully. Moreover, project work requires certain skills that have often never been taught and most of which have to be learned along the way. However, despite the effort and sometimes the pain of this type of learning, these skills are immediately transferable to most 'knowledge-based' jobs, and can provide a valuable boost to confidence.

We hope that you have enjoyed the book and found it useful. For our part, we look forward to many more years of involvement with student-researchers as they undertake their information systems research projects.

Index